Quick Guide to Community Care Practice and the Law

by the same author

Community Care Practice and the Law
Fourth edition
ISBN 978 1 84310 691 3

Safeguarding Vulnerable Adults and the Law
ISBN 978 1 84310 692 0

Manual Handling in Health and Social Care
An A-Z of Law and Practice
ISBN 978 1 84310 041 6

QUICK GUIDE

TO

COMMUNITY CARE

PRACTICE AND

THE LAW

MICHAEL MANDELSTAM

Jessica Kingsley Publishers
London and Philadelphia

First published in 2010
by Jessica Kingsley Publishers
116 Pentonville Road
London N1 9JB, UK
and
400 Market Street, Suite 400
Philadelphia, PA 19106, USA

www.jkp.com

Library of Congress Cataloging in Publication Data
A CIP catalog record for this book is available from the Library of Congress

British Library Cataloguing in Publication Data
A CIP catalogue record for this book is available from the British Library

ISBN 978 1 84905 083 8

Printed and bound in Great Britain by
MPG Books Limited

Contents

Preface

During the 1980s, I had the good fortune to work with Mrs Sheila Holden, a retired senior civil servant who had worked previously at the Department of Health. She was now assisting in a voluntary capacity at the Disabled Living Foundation. She taught me the importance of giving people proper information about legislation and government guidance. Even back then, the system was complicated. Now, not only is it even *more* complex, but both central and local government have contrived unintentionally – or otherwise, one sometimes suspects – to make it, arguably, impenetrable.

I have therefore written this book in the hope of providing a short, readable and useful guide to community care law. However, brevity poses a dilemma. Full exposition and illustration of the rules produce a large volume – some 650 pages, in the case of the parent of this book.[1] Equally, too broad a brush defeats the object of providing a sufficiently sharp, *practical* tool, which can be used to examine, question and challenge policies and decisions.

A degree of selectivity is inevitably involved. I make no apologies; the somewhat clichéd expression comes to mind about the best sometimes being the enemy of the good. I have focused on those issues that seem most regularly to give rise to confusion and misapplication of the law. In addition, it is intended that some topics will be expanded upon further within this *Quick Guides* series.

Nonetheless, references are listed at the foot of each page, so that the reader can delve further. These days, many of the references are found easily on the internet. They are included by way of evidence for what I have written. But they are also there for credibility generally. Without them, the unwary reader might be tempted to conclude that I have written a fantastical and elaborate work of fiction – such is the

---

1   Mandelstam, M. (2009) *Community Care Practice and the Law.* 4th edition. London: Jessica Kingsley Publishers.

labyrinthine, chaotic and opaque nature of community care law, policy and practice.

ACKNOWLEDGEMENTS

My thanks are due, as ever, to Jessica Kingsley for her longstanding, unstinting support and encouragement, and to her staff. More generally, Pauline Thompson and Simon Bull continue generously to share their great expertise and to keep me up to the mark. Where I have fallen short in this book, and mistakes are probably inevitable, it is entirely my responsibility and fault. All views expressed are my own, unless attributed otherwise.

CHAPTER 1

Introduction

- Community care services
- Regulation of services
- National Health Service
- Home adaptations
- Mental capacity, human rights, discrimination, health and safety at work, negligence

This book concerns the law and practice of community care. More precisely, it is about social care, health care and some housing services provided for certain groups of people who need help or assistance. These groups include older people with various needs and disabilities, younger adults with disabilities (physical, sensory or learning), people with mental health needs, and people with drug or alcohol problems. Also covered are the informal carers of such people, including family and friends. The book is mostly about adults, although some of the legal rules and principles covered apply to children as well.

COMMUNITY CARE SERVICES

Community care services, as defined in legislation, relate to what is generally called 'social care' provided by local social services authorities. That is, local councils with social services responsibilities.[1] These are unitary councils of one type or another (e.g. borough or metropolitan councils) or county councils, whose role it is to assess whether people need these services.

This community care legislation comprises over ten different Acts of Parliament stretching as far back as sixty years. It lists a myriad of

---

1 *Local Authority Social Services Act 1970*, schedule 1.

services including residential and nursing care in care homes, personal care in people's own homes, home help with household tasks, 'respite care' (giving people breaks from caring), holidays, equipment to make life easier in people's homes (e.g. raised toilet seat, perching stool, special cutlery), adapting people's homes (e.g. grab rails, ramps, stairlifts), meals-on-wheels, day centres, recreational activities, and so on. In short, the range of help that local authorities can provide is substantial.

Within this legal framework of assessment and services are two policies in particular that warrant mention. The first is about protecting or safeguarding vulnerable adults from abuse and neglect. The second is called 'personalisation' or self-directed support, whereby people are given personal budgets with which they can organise their own care.

REGULATION OF SERVICES

Over the past decade, the regulation of community care and health care services has assumed greater prominence, roughly in proportion to the increased amount of care being contracted out by local authorities and NHS bodies to independent providers of care. Such regulation is about trying to ensure that services are provided at least to a minimum standard. An independent commission, the Care Quality Commission, is now responsible for the registration and inspection of all community care and health care providers, including National Health Service bodies.

NATIONAL HEALTH SERVICE

As well as social care services, community care in the general sense involves also health and nursing care provided by the National Health Service (NHS). This may be provided, for example, in people's own homes, in care homes or in community hospitals. Even admissions to, discharges from and standards of care in acute hospitals are linked inextricably to community care.

HOME ADAPTATIONS

Adaptations to disabled people's homes can be provided not only by local councils with social services responsibilities, but also – and under separate legislation – by councils with housing responsibilities. These are unitary councils of one type or another (e.g. borough or metropolitan councils) or district councils. Adaptations can enable people either to remain, or to remain more independently, in their own homes.

MENTAL CAPACITY, HUMAN RIGHTS, DISCRIMINATION, HEALTH AND SAFETY AT WORK, NEGLIGENCE

Other legislation relevant to community care includes the Mental Capacity Act 2005, Human Rights Act 1998, Disability Discrimination Act 1995, health and safety at work legislation and the common law of negligence.

CHAPTER 2

How community care law and practice works

- Lack of scrutiny and debate in community care
- A morass of legislation
- Unfairness
- Two-faced policies
- Cheerleading to cover the gap between policy and practice
- Practical ill consequences of the gap between policy and practice
    - The gap between fine-sounding words and available resources
    - Shortcuts taken by local authorities
    - Shortcuts taken by the National Health Service

SUMMARY

Understanding the legal rules of community care is difficult because of their complexity, obscurity and contradictions. Even such an understanding is insufficient to shed light on how community care really works, because in practice the rules are often not adhered to. This is partly because of their complexity but also because the aspiration of underlying policy has become increasingly divorced from what can realistically be achieved. In turn, this leads to disingenuousness on the part of central government, local authorities and NHS bodies, and to shortcuts being taken. Some of these shortcuts are lawful, some not, and some are highly detrimental to people's welfare. Uncertainty and ambiguity are consequently endemic.

LACK OF SCRUTINY AND DEBATE IN COMMUNITY CARE
Uncertainty is further fuelled when new policies in social and health care are implemented by the backdoor. For instance, two major policies in community care, safeguarding adults and 'personalisation', have been introduced with no explicit underlying legislation – and thus with no formal debate, scrutiny and approval by Parliament. In principle, such an omission is suspect. Consequently, these policies occupy a legislative no-man's land and create uncertainty; nobody quite knows what is or *should be* going on. Likewise, controversially, the longstanding unspoken policy of running down 'NHS continuing health care' – and thereby forcing people to pay for care that used to be free of charge – has been implemented with a lack of transparency and with no explicit legislation or formal public debate.

A MORASS OF LEGISLATION
Even when policy has more properly been debated and turned into legislation, matters do not proceed straightforwardly. The relevant bit of the NHS and Community Act 1990 was inserted and passed in haste, without proper consideration and consolidation of existing community care legislation – some of it dating back as far as 1948. The Department of Health was nervous about such consolidation, for fear that it would expose too glaringly the problems and contradictions of the new legislation. The resulting legislative morass was foreseeable; the many Acts of Parliament now making up community care do not cohere and are difficult to understand. In 2009, the Law Commission condemned the existing system as 'inadequate, often incomprehensible and outdated'.[1]

UNFAIRNESS
The community care system is regarded as unfair and chaotic. Some people, increasingly fewer, qualify for totally free 'continuing care' from the NHS. Others have to pay local authorities (or go private) for all their personal and social care, assuming they have a certain level of

---

1   Law Commission (2008) *Adult Social Care: Scoping Report.* London: Law Commission, p.129.

financial assets. This penalises those who have worked hard to build up modest means, but who then become rapidly impoverished by disability or illness.[2] In addition, ever more people, irrespective of their financial assets, anyway don't qualify for assistance at all because of stricter 'eligibility' rules applied by local authorities. Yet even this depends on where a person lives: some authorities are more generous than others. In July 2009, central government belatedly conceded that the system is unfair; it published a Green Paper in order to consult about how a future 'national care system' could operate and social care costs be spread between the government and individuals.[3]

TWO-FACED POLICIES

Policies in community care and health are often two faced. The public face is the attractive one. It talks of the good practice and the good services we all intuitively want. The other, more shadowy, is about containing expenditure, ruthlessly if need be. This state of affairs creates an obvious tension. Local authorities and NHS bodies seek to minimise expenditure and avoid providing services, while laying claim to being caring and compassionate. Consequently, they are drawn magnetically to shortcuts – some crude, some sophisticated and some unlawful. Such corner cutting is widespread, since social care is significantly under-funded[4]; the Care Quality Commission stated in 2009 that it expected this to worsen in the light of pressure on public spending.[5]

CHEERLEADING TO COVER THE GAP BETWEEN POLICY AND PRACTICE

Notwithstanding this gap between policy and practice, the central government of the day tends to produce a wealth of information and publicity trumpeting the policy. Green Papers are covered with uniformly smiling faces and filled with uplifting and aspirational prose.[6] Unsurprisingly, everybody's expectations are raised. A situation develops where inflated claims are made about a policy, while what is actually provided – at least for significant numbers of people – is quite

---

2   Dickson, N. (2007) 'Is this the answer to the age-old question of social care funding?' *Health Service Journal 117*, 16–17.
3   Secretary of State for Health (2009) *Shaping the Future of Care Together*. Cm 7673. London: TSO.
4   Wanless, D. (2006) *Securing Good Care for Older People: Taking a Long Term View*. London: King's Fund.
5   Rose, D. 'Care homes come under pressure to cut costs.' *The Times*, 1 April 2009.
6   Secretary of State for Health (2009) *Shaping the Future of Care Together*. Cm 7673. London: TSO.

different. A vicious circle takes shape. In order to bridge the increasing gap, central government, local authorities and NHS bodies make ever greater, sometimes absurd, claims and promises. Perversely, the greater the failure of a policy, the more extravagant tend to be the claims made about it.

PRACTICAL ILL CONSEQUENCES OF THE GAP BETWEEN POLICY AND PRACTICE

The consequences of the gap between policy and practice are not theoretical. They have a serious impact on people who need help and who may not get it, as illustrated immediately below.

Also affected are those professionals, staff and managers in local authorities and NHS bodies whose daily working lives are too often fraught with anxiety, fear and professional doubts about what they find themselves caught up in. They are aware that to speak out may result in their being victimised in one way or another. Yet not speaking out contributes to an acceptance of poor practice.

THE GAP BETWEEN FINE-SOUNDING WORDS AND AVAILABLE RESOURCES

At a general level, the law courts had by 1997 pointed out the gap between the fine-sounding words of government community care policy and the everyday reality of insufficient resources. This was in the context of a local authority trying to withdraw services from 1500 vulnerable elderly people.[7] Since then, the majority of community care legal cases have concerned the mismatch between resources and people's needs.

For people who need help, the consequences of the gap are serious. Over a ten-year period between 1997 and 2007, local authorities ended up helping 25 per cent fewer people. In other words, and despite the rhetoric, ever fewer people who need help actually get it. The official policy under which this has been achieved is called 'fair access to care'. It is a classic example of how a fair-sounding policy conceals something rather different. This reduction in assistance for people in need has been condemned, by the government's own inspectorate, as leading to a serious erosion of older people's dignity, welfare and physical safety.[8] In

---

7   R v Gloucestershire County Council, ex p Barry [1997] 2 All ER 1, House of Lords.
8   See generally: Henwood, M. and Hudson, B. (2008) Lost to the System? The Impact of Fair Access to Care. London: CSCI. Also: Commission for Social Care Inspection (2008) The State of Social Care in England 2006–07. London: CSCI.

addition, even when local authorities do still provide help, it is too often insufficient and so people still have to buy in extra care privately.[9]

SHORTCUTS TAKEN BY LOCAL AUTHORITIES

Local authorities explore all manner of shortcuts in order to minimise their responsibilities and expenditure. For example, they manipulate 'eligibility' rules about what needs will qualify for services. They attempt to avoid assessing people, either at all or properly. They will not always meet needs even when there is a duty to do so. And they do not baulk at charging people for services against the rules. They sometimes make up rules that are far removed from any basis in law.

The pressure on local authorities has recently manifested itself in the form of 'reverse bid' internet auctions for the care of older people. This involves online bidding for contracts, to see which provider can deliver the cheapest care for older people.[10] In similar vein, having contracted out services to independent providers, local authorities tend to neglect properly to monitor and review performance of the contract – even when this leads to the death of vulnerable people.[11] For central government (in power or in waiting), the trend seems to be that everything – including frail older people – has its price and can be sold as a cut-price commodity. As one Shadow Minister put it, in relation to reorganising and contracting out local authority services, 'assessment is pretty much the same whether you are assessing pot holes or assessing care for the elderly'.[12]

At the time of writing, local authorities are implementing the policy of personalisation and self-directed support mentioned above. The idea is to give people more choice, control and independence over how their needs are met; rhetoric from government paints a bright new future. Few would argue with the principles here; but it is almost certain that authorities will from the outset undermine them by treating the policy primarily as a cost-saving measure. Already anecdotal evidence is emerging of how, even in the earliest days of this new policy, local

---

9   Forder, J. (2007) *Self-funded Care for Older People: An Analysis of Eligibility, Variations and Future Projections.* London: CSCI, pp.5–9.

10 *BBC News.* 'Britain's home care scandal', 9 April 2009. Available at: www.news.bbc.co.uk/programmes/600jnknl, accessed on 17 August 2009.

11 E.g. local government ombudsman investigations: *Sheffield City Council 2007* (05/C/06420). Also: *Liverpool City Council 2007* (05/C/08592).

12 Sherman, J. and Hamilton, F. 'Councils poised to hand running of care and education to private firms.' *The Times,* 4 March 2009.

authorities are exploring ways of discriminating against older people – the largest group of community care users of services.[13]

SHORTCUTS TAKEN BY THE NATIONAL HEALTH SERVICE

Likewise in the NHS, despite the immense amount of official publicity to the contrary, patients – in particular, older people – may in certain circumstances experience a desperately poor quality of care as a result of any number of shortcuts taken.

This may typically be associated with systematic and deliberate over-occupancy of hospital beds, understaffing, the placing of targets and statistics ahead of humane patient care and concealment – and a culture of fear and bullying within the NHS. This is not over-statement. All these issues have been identified over the past few years by the Healthcare Commission as significant, contributory factors to appalling standards of care, to gross indignities suffered by patients and – even in a single hospital – to infection and scores of avoidable deaths. The Commission – before it was wound up unceremoniously by the government in March 2009 – emphasised that such issues are a common problem within the NHS.[14]

Yet, trapped by its own rhetoric, central government continues in denial. For instance, it largely and instantly dismissed a Patients' Association report in August 2009 about poor care in hospitals. This was despite the fact that the report triggered widespread public reaction to, and recognition of, what the Association had found[15] – and that it merely echoed the repeated findings and warnings of the Healthcare Commission.

Another significant shortcut has been the running down of rehabilitation services, particularly for older people with more complex needs (as opposed to those with simpler needs that can be met by shorter term reablement and intermediate care). The number of rehabilitation beds, in both acute and community hospitals, has fallen significantly.[16]

---

13 Ahmed, M. 'Older people receive less money than young adults.' *Community Care 8*, 21 May 2009.

14 Healthcare Commission (2006) *Investigation into Outbreaks of Clostridium Difficile at Stoke Mandeville Hospital, Buckinghamshire Hospitals NHS Trust*. London: HC, Healthcare Commission (2007) *Investigation into Outbreaks of Clostridium Difficile at Maidstone and Tunbridge Wells NHS Trust*. London: HC, Healthcare Commission (2009) *Investigation into Mid Staffordshire NHS Foundation Trust*. London: HC.

15 Patients' Association (2009) *Patients not Numbers, People not Statistics*. London: PA. And: Smith, R. '"Cruel and neglectful" care of one million NHS patients exposed.' *Daily Telegraph*, 27 August 2009. And: Rayner, C. 'Tough love for the NHS.' *The Guardian*, 28 August 2009.

16 British Geriatric Society (2007) *Rehabilitation Beds Report on the Second England Council Survey*. London: BGS.

Furthermore, and straddling health and social care, is the vexed issue of NHS continuing health care. This is about whether the NHS should pay for a person's continuing care needs (in which case it is free of charge) or whether local authorities should be responsible (in which case people have to pay, and even sell their homes, in order to do so). This issue has epitomised the lack of logic, transparency and fairness that afflicts the community care system generally.[17]

---

17 Health Service Ombudsman (2004) *NHS Funding for Long Term Care.* London: TSO.

CHAPTER 3

When things go wrong

- Members of Parliament, local councillors, newspapers
- Local authority monitoring officers
- Local authority and NHS complaints procedures
  - Overall duties
  - Who can make a complaint?
  - Complaints that do not have to be dealt with
  - Dealing with complaints across more than one organisation
  - Care standards complaints
  - Time limit on making a complaint
  - Responding to the complaint
  - Remedies
- Intervention by the Secretary of State
- Local authority and health service ombudsmen
  - Maladministration and failure to provide services
  - Joint investigations by the ombudsmen
  - Investigating contracted-out services
  - Ombudsman recommendations and enforcement
  - Remedies from the ombudsmen
- Independent complaints advocacy service
- Access to general and personal information
  - General information
  - Personal information
  - Data Protection Act 1998
- Basic legal principles
  - What a duty is
  - Directions, approvals and guidance

- Judicial-review legal cases: what the courts look for
  - Rigid policies: fettering of discretion
  - Taking account of relevant factors and unreasonableness
  - Illegality: breach of duty and blatant contravention of legislation
  - Legitimate expectations and consultation
  - Giving reasons
  - Permission and time limits to bringing a judicial review case
  - Who can bring a judicial review case?
  - Whether to bring a complaint or a legal case?

SUMMARY

It is not much good knowing about the law without knowing what can be done if things go wrong. Informal remedies, formal complaints and legal action are all possibilities. Clearly not everybody can or wants to complain; still fewer people are in any sort of position to bring legal action. The hope is that local authorities and the NHS would make efforts to ensure that they adhere to the law and to good administration – thus diminishing the need for complaints or legal cases. However, this hope cannot necessarily be relied on.

MEMBERS OF PARLIAMENT, LOCAL COUNCILLORS, NEWSPAPERS

MPs and local councillors might take up the cases of constituents for benevolent, compassionate or political reasons. Going to the local or national newspapers is sometimes effective.

LOCAL AUTHORITY MONITORING OFFICERS

Local authority monitoring officers (each authority is obliged to have one) have a duty to report on actual or potential contraventions of legislation or associated codes of practice, and on any actual or possible maladministration or injustice caused by the authority.[1] It may be worth raising matters with them, in order to bring pressure on a local authority that appears to be taking unlawful shortcuts.

---

1   *Local Government and Housing Act 1989,* s.5.

LOCAL AUTHORITY AND NHS COMPLAINTS PROCEDURES

Local authority and NHS complaints procedures are, in principle at least, suitable for most grievances. Complaints procedures should be speedy but may in practice be protracted. They are, anyway, not appropriate for resolving points of law. The local government ombudsman has published a useful guide about the good administration of complaints procedures.[2] Since April 2009, a common set of rules covers social services and NHS complaints procedures, as well as those of independent health and social care providers. In summary, the rules, under the regulations, are as follows.[3]

OVERALL DUTIES

Each 'responsible body' – a local authority, NHS body or independent provider – must have a complaints procedure, and it must provide information about the procedure. Complaints must be dealt with efficiently and investigated properly. Complainants must be treated respectfully and courteously, receive assistance to help them understand the complaints procedure, receive a timely and appropriate response, and be informed of the outcome of the complaint. The responsible body must take action where necessary in response to the complaint. Each responsible body must appoint somebody to ensure overall compliance with the complaints regulations, and also a complaints manager.

WHO CAN MAKE A COMPLAINT?

Complaints can be made by:

(a) anybody who has received services from the responsible body

(b) somebody affected by the subject matter of the complaint

(c) somebody else acting on behalf of a person who has died, of a child, of somebody who lacks capacity to complain, or

(d) somebody else at the request of the service user.

COMPLAINTS THAT DO NOT HAVE TO BE DEALT WITH

Some complaints don't have formally to be investigated; for example, complaints made orally and resolved within a day, complaints previously

---

2   Local Government Ombudsman (2008) *Guidance on Running a Complaints System.* London: LGO.
3   SI 2009/309. *The Local Authority Social Services and National Health Service Complaints (England) Regulations 2009.* Made under the: *Health and Social Care (Community Health and Standards) Act 2003.*

investigated, or complaints related to the Freedom of Information Act 2000.

DEALING WITH COMPLAINTS ACROSS MORE THAN ONE ORGANISATION

A local authority must deal with complaints about its discharge of its social services functions. It must also deal with complaints when it has arranged for services to be provided by somebody else – and also when it is providing services on behalf of the NHS. (Likewise, the NHS must deal with complaints about services it is providing on behalf of a local authority.)

Primary care providers (e.g. general medical practitioners) and independent care providers must deal with complaints when they are providing services on behalf of the NHS. When NHS primary care trusts receive a complaint, they can either deal with it themselves or – with the complainant's consent – decide whether it is more appropriate for the provider to deal with it.

If a complaint applies to more than one responsible body, then the two bodies must coordinate the handling of the complaint and ensure that the complainant receives a coordinated response.

CARE STANDARDS COMPLAINTS

If a local authority receives a complaint that is either partly or wholly about 'care standards', it must ask the complainant whether he or she consents to details of the complaint being sent to the care provider. A care standards complaint is where the complaint is about provision by a care provider registered under the Care Standards Act 2000 (or, in future, the Health and Social Care Act 2008), but is not directly to do with the local authority. When the complaint is partly to do with the local authority and partly the care provider, the local authority must cooperate with the care provider to ensure a coordinated response to the complaint. Similar rules apply to a complaint (a) about a 'social care provider', defined as a provider of adult social care, and (b) not to do with the local authority.

TIME LIMIT ON MAKING A COMPLAINT

A complaint must be made within 12 months of the event being complained of – unless there are good reasons for the delay and the complaint can still be investigated effectively and fairly.

RESPONDING TO THE COMPLAINT

Complaints can be made orally or in writing. Even oral complaints must be recorded in writing. Generally, the complaint must be acknowledged within three days. The responsible body must offer to discuss how the complaint should be handled, and how long it is likely to take.

The responsible body must investigate the complaint speedily and efficiently, and keep the complainant informed of progress. As soon as practicable, the responsible body must send the complainant a written response, including:

(a) a report covering how the complaint has been considered, conclusions and any remedial action

(b) confirmation that any necessary action has been taken

(c) the complainant's right to take the complaint further, either to the local ombudsman or the health service ombudsman (in the case of local authority or NHS-related complaints).

If a written response has not been sent within six months, the responsible body must tell the complainant in writing why, and send a response as soon as practicable.

REMEDIES

Local authorities have the power to remedy injustice arising from a complaint. This can include both financial and non-financial redress.[4]

INTERVENTION BY THE SECRETARY OF STATE

If a local authority or NHS body fails to perform its duties, the Secretary of State can declare it to be in default.[5] It seems that these powers have not been used formally, which would suggest this is a hollow remedy.

LOCAL AUTHORITY AND HEALTH SERVICE OMBUDSMEN

The local government ombudsmen (there are three in England) independently investigate complaints against local authorities, normally when the local authority's complaints procedure has been exhausted but the complainant wishes to take the complaint further.[6] The health

---

4   *Local Government Act 2000*, s.92.
5   *Local Authority Social Services Act 1970*, s.7D; *NHS Act 2006*, s.68.
6   *Local Government Act 1974*.

service ombudsman, of whom there is one in England, does the same in respect of the NHS.[7]

MALADMINISTRATION AND FAILURE TO PROVIDE SERVICES

The local ombudsmen can investigate a complaint about maladministration, failure in a service that there was a duty to provide, and failure to provide such a service. Maladministration can cover a wide range of issues.[8] The health service ombudsman likewise; and although he or she is not able to question the merits of decisions, he or she can question clinical judgement.[9]

JOINT INVESTIGATIONS BY THE OMBUDSMEN

The local ombudsman and health service ombudsman are able to share information and run joint investigations.[10] This power is particularly relevant to health and social care, given increased joint working between the NHS and local authorities. For instance, just such a joint investigation took place when both the NHS and local authority were involved in the failure properly to assess and to meet the needs of a man with learning disabilities in a care home.[11]

INVESTIGATING CONTRACTED-OUT SERVICES

The local government ombudsman investigates local authorities; however, increasingly, authorities are contracting out community care services to the independent sector. So, the legislation makes clear that when a local authority does this, the actions of the contractor are to be treated as actions of the local authority and so are subject to investigation by the ombudsman.[12] The health service ombudsman can do likewise in relation to the NHS.[13] From October 2010, the law is due to change so that the local ombudsman will be able to investigate complaints against independent sector providers – even when the complainant has made a purely private arrangement with the provider.[14]

7   *Health Service Commissioners Act 1993.*

8   Commission for Local Administration in England (1993) *Good Administrative Practice.* London: CLAE.

9   *Health Service Commissioners Act 1993,* s.3.

10   *Local Government Act 1974; Parliamentary Commissioner Act 1967;* and *Health Service Commissioner's Act 1993:* all as amended by SI 2007/1889.

11   *Buckinghamshire County Council and Oxfordshire & Buckinghamshire Mental Health Partnership Trust 2008* (03/1/04618 local ombudsman, and HS-2608 health service ombudsman).

12   *Local Government Act 1974,* s.25.

13   *Health Service Commissioners Act 1993,* s.2B.

14   *Health Act 2009,* s.35

OMBUDSMAN RECOMMENDATIONS AND ENFORCEMENT

Local authorities are not obliged to comply with recommendations of the local ombudsmen but must consider them. If a council refuses to follow the ombudsman's recommendations, even after a second report, it can be forced to publish an agreed statement in a local newspaper at its own expense.[15] Avoidance of bad publicity is thus an additional incentive for local authorities; non-compliance is rare.[16] Similarly, health service ombudsman recommendations are not binding on the NHS.

REMEDIES FROM THE OMBUDSMEN

When maladministration has caused injustice, the local ombudsmen can recommend any lawful remedy, including financial compensation.[17] Recommendations typically include the local authority providing the disputed service, apologising or rewriting policies to avoid future recurrence of the maladministration. On matters of wider importance, the ombudsmen sometimes write to the Department of Health.

Financial compensation recommended by the local ombudsman typically ranges from £500 to £5000. It can be more; for instance, as much as £80,000 or £100,000 when the parents of disabled adults incurred financial loss because of the local authority's failures – having to give up their jobs[18] or pay for care.[19]

The health service ombudsman tends not to award financial compensation as much as the local ombudsman does, but may do so, for instance, where a person has wrongly had to pay for care that should have been free of charge through the NHS.[20]

INDEPENDENT COMPLAINTS ADVOCACY SERVICE

There is a duty on the NHS to arrange provision of independent advocacy services (ICAS) to assist individuals to make complaints against the NHS. The duty extends as far as is considered necessary to meet all reasonable requirements.[21] In addition is a non-statutory service called Patient Advice and Liaison Services (PALS), to provide

15 *Local Government Act 1974*, s.31.
16 Commission for Local Administration in England (2004) *Local Government Ombudsman: Annual Report 2003/4.* London: CLAE, p.30.
17 *Local Government Act 1974*, s.31.
18 *Trafford Metropolitan Borough Council 2007* (05/C/11921) and (05/C/11921).
19 *Hertfordshire County Council 2003* (01/B/09360).
20 *North Worcestershire Health Authority 1995* (E.264/94–95). In: Health Service Commissioner (1995) HC 11. *Selected Investigations Completed April to September 1995.* London: HMSO.
21 *National Health Service Act 2006*, s.248.

confidential advice and support to patients, their families and carers in resolving problems and concerns quickly.[22]

ACCESS TO GENERAL AND PERSONAL INFORMATION

It may be essential for those bringing complaints or legal cases to get hold of relevant information. In addition, local authority and NHS staff may need to share information, sometimes without a person's consent – for instance, in relation to safeguarding or adult protection matters.

GENERAL INFORMATION

In order to explore possible grounds of complaint or challenge to a decision, an individual might need general information – for example, about a council's policy. The Freedom of Information Act 2000 means that public bodies – such as local authorities and NHS bodies – must have a publication scheme and provide information, generally non-personal, in response to requests. There are various exempted types of information. In addition, the NHS is subject to a code of practice on openness.[23]

PERSONAL INFORMATION

The law generally affecting the holding and sharing of personal information includes the common law of confidentiality, the Data Protection Act 1998 and article 8 of the European Convention on Human Rights (article 8 refers to people's right to respect for their private life).

The common law (i.e. not in legislation but developed by the courts) of confidentiality may apply to any particular issue not covered specifically by other legislation. It is about balancing the private and pubic interests of confidentiality against the private and public interests of disclosure. For instance, it might concern disclosure by a doctor to a hospital about a mental health patient,[24] by a local authority to a mother of her son's health and social care files,[25] by the police to a regulatory body about the death of a resident in nursing home,[26] or by a local authority to a care home about child-care proceedings taken

---

22 Secretary of State for Health (2000) The NHS Plan. London: TSO, para 10.17.
23 Department of Health (2003) Code of Practice on Openness in the NHS. London: DH.
24 W v Edgell [1990] 1 All ER 835, Court of Appeal.
25 R v Plymouth City Council, ex p Stevens [2002] EWCA Civ 388.
26 Woolgar v Chief Constable of Sussex Police (2000) 1 WLR 25, Court of Appeal.

against a woman working at the care home.[27] The courts have generally expected the disclosing organisation to justify disclosure by carrying out a 'pressing need' test.[28]

DATA PROTECTION ACT 1998

The Data Protection Act 1998 contains a number of key points, including 'data protection principles', which are relevant to the processing – for example, obtaining, holding, sharing, destroying – of personal information. Broadly they are about maintaining the balance between confidentiality and disclosure.

The Act also creates a presumption that people will have access to their own personal information, subject to certain safeguards where harm might be caused by disclosure.[29] For instance, such safeguards might justify a mental health patient being denied access to a psychology report that was being submitted to a mental-health review tribunal hearing.[30] There are also provisos where the information sought contains information about third parties – that is, people other than the data subject.

BASIC LEGAL PRINCIPLES

Local authorities and NHS bodies are legal animals; they exist only by virtue of legislation. The legislation brings them into existence and confers functions on them. Duties are functions that must be carried out. Powers are basically discretionary. Confusingly, some duties are stronger than others and therefore easier to enforce; and powers may be weak but should not be ignored.

If their policies, practices and decisions are inconsistent with legislation, then public bodies will go wrong in law. This makes it important to know what the law actually says about duties and powers.

WHAT A DUTY IS

Duties are generally indicated by words such as 'shall' or 'must'. Some duties are relatively weak. They are general or 'target' in nature, owed

---

27 *Brent LBC v SK* [2007] EWHC 1250, Fam.
28 *R v Chief Constable of North Wales, ex p AB* [1998] 3 WLR 57, Court of Appeal.
29 *Data Protection 1998*, s.7, schedules 1–3. See also: SI 2000/413. *Data Protection (Subject Access Modification) (Health) Order 2000*. And: SI 2000/415. *Data Protection (Subject Access Modification) (Social Work) Order 2000*.
30 *Roberts v Nottinghamshire Healthcare NHS Trust* [2008] EWHC 1934, Queen's Bench.

to the (local) population at large rather than each individual person. As such they are difficult to enforce.[31] Such weak duties underpin, for instance, the provision of most NHS services.[32] Other duties are regarded as specific duties towards individual people and are easier to enforce; for instance, providing community care services in people's own homes or residential accommodation.[33]

DIRECTIONS, APPROVALS AND GUIDANCE

Apart from legislation, there are also 'directions' and 'approvals', which are made under legislation. They create duties and powers respectively. In addition, there is the huge quantity of guidance issued by the Department of Health to local authorities and to the NHS.

For local social services authorities, there are two types of guidance, stronger and weaker. Stronger guidance is sometimes called 'statutory' or 'policy' guidance. It is made under s.7 of the Local Authority Social Services Act 1970. This Act places a duty on local authorities to act under the general guidance of the Secretary of State. Such guidance must generally be followed by local authorities.[34] Codes of practice have a similar status, such as those for the Mental Health Act 1983 and the Mental Capacity Act 2005.[35] Even weaker guidance must be taken account of,[36] and should not be simply binned, metaphorically or otherwise. The problems with the guidance are several-fold. There is far too much of it, involving huge time, effort and resources in local implementation. It is of variable quality, some guidance contradicts other guidance, and it is sometimes barely consistent with the law.

For the NHS, there is no formal distinction between stronger (statutory) and weaker guidance. Even so, a failure to take proper account of guidance may still be unlawful.[37]

---

31 *R v Inner London Education Authority (ILEA), ex p Ali* [1990] 2 ALR 822.

32 *R v Cambridge Health Authority, ex p B* [1995] 6 MLR 250, Court of Appeal.

33 *R v Gloucestershire County Council, ex p Barry* [1997] 2 All ER 1, House of Lords; *R v Sefton Metropolitan Borough Council, ex p Help the Aged* [1997] 3 FCR 573, Court of Appeal.

34 *Robertson v Fife Council* [2002] UKHL 35, House of Lords.

35 Department of Health (2008) *Code of Practice: Mental Health Act 1983.* London: TSO; Lord Chancellor (2007) *Mental Capacity Act 2005: Code of Practice.* London: TSO.

36 *R v Islington London Borough Council, ex p Rixon* [1997] 1 ELR 477.

37 *R v North Derbyshire Health Authority, ex p Fisher* [1998] 8 MLR 327.

JUDICIAL-REVIEW LEGAL CASES: WHAT THE COURTS LOOK FOR

Law stems from the decisions of the law courts as well as legislation. In particular, judicial-review legal cases are central to community care and health care. They involve the courts applying common law principles to test the fairness of decisions taken by, and only by, public bodies.

Judicial review is sometimes referred to as supervisory: it is about ensuring that public bodies stay roughly on the rails. However, the courts don't want to step right into the shoes of the public body. So, if a local authority or an NHS body has made an unlawful decision, the court usually orders it to go away and retake it – this time in a lawful manner – rather than saying exactly what the outcome of the decision should be. Next time round, the local authority or NHS body might still reach the same conclusion as it did before, but this time on the 'right' grounds. In other words, judicial review is more about the process of decision-making, rather than the final outcome.

The upshot is that the courts sometimes appear excessively deferential to local authorities and the NHS (for instance, allowing care homes to be closed and highly vulnerable residents moved out);[38] at other times they intervene more boldly (for example, ensuring that 95-year-old women get a proper and fair assessment).[39]

RIGID POLICIES: FETTERING OF DISCRETION

The courts (and ombudsmen) may react against policies applied so inflexibly that exceptions cannot be taken account of. This is called 'fettering of discretion' and should be avoided. At the very least, the courts may look hard to see whether there was a genuine mechanism for the making of exceptions. For instance, they have found against local authorities because of rigid policies on holidays,[40] financial ceilings on care packages[41] – and against the NHS in respect of gender reassignment surgery[42] and cancer treatment.[43]

---

38 R(Cowl) v Plymouth CC [2001] EWCA Civ 1935; R(Compton) v Wiltshire Primary Care Trust [2009] EWHC 1824 Admin.

39 R(Goldsmith) v Wandsworth London Borough Council [2004] EWCA Civ 1170; R v North and East Devon Health Authority, ex p Coughlan (1999) 2 CCLR 285, Court of Appeal.

40 R v North Yorkshire County Council, ex p Hargreaves (no.2) [1997] 96 LGR 39.

41 R(Alloway) v Bromley London Borough Council [2004] EWHC 2108 (Admin).

42 R v North West Lancashire Health Authority, ex p G,A,D (1999) 2 CCLR 419, Court of Appeal.

43 R(Rogers) v Swindon NHS Primary Care Trust [2006] EWCA Civ 392; R(Otley) v Barking and Dagenham Primary Care Trust [2007] EWHC Admin 1927.

TAKING ACCOUNT OF RELEVANT FACTORS AND UNREASONABLENESS

In the context of community care, the courts sometimes scrutinise assessment decisions, to ensure that all relevant factors have been taken account of – for instance, psychological issues,[44] cultural and language issues,[45] medical factors,[46] people's preferences (as demanded by Department of Health guidance),[47] and health and safety of staff.[48] This principle has also been applied to NHS decision-making, for example, when a primary care trust failed to take account of whether a cancer drug would prolong the patient's life for more than a few months.[49]

Occasionally, even if all relevant factors have been considered, the courts might rule that a decision is simply too outlandish to stand. When a local authority decided that a person attending a day centre could afford to pay – but only by using part of a disability benefit that was being received for night-time care – this was deemed irrational.[50] Likewise an NHS trust's policy on cancer drugs which were denied to a patient. The trust had equated exceptionality, the ground in its policy for providing the drug, with uniqueness – a much stricter and virtually unattainable notion. In addition, relevant clinical and cost-effectiveness factors had not been taken account of.[51]

ILLEGALITY: BREACH OF DUTY AND BLATANT CONTRAVENTION OF LEGISLATION

Sometimes local authorities explicitly breach duties set out in legislation. For example, in one case a local authority made up its own rules for charging people for residential care, even though the rules were prescribed by legislation.[52]

LEGITIMATE EXPECTATIONS AND CONSULTATION

The courts sometimes consider whether people's 'legitimate expectations' have been observed. Such expectations are generally about a *procedural*

---

44 *R v Avon County Council, ex p M* [1994] 2 FCR 259.
45 *R(Khana) v Southwark London Borough Council* [2001] EWCA Civ 999, Court of Appeal.
46 *R v Birmingham City Council, ex p Killigrew* (2000) 3 CCLR 109. Also: *R(Clegg) v Salford City Council* [2007] EWHC 3276 Admin.
47 *R v North Yorkshire County Council, ex p Hargreaves* [1994] 26 BMLR 121.
48 *R v Cornwall County Council, ex p Goldsack* (1996) unreported. Also: *R(A&B, X&Y) v East Sussex County Council (no.2)* [2003] EWHC Admin 167.
49 *R(Otley) v Barking and Dagenham Primary Care Trust* [2007] EWHC Admin 1927.
50 *R(Carton) v Coventry City Council* (2001) 4 CCLR 41.
51 *R(Ross) v West Sussex Primary Care Trust* [2008] EWHC 2252 Admin.
52 *R v Sefton Metropolitan Borough Council, ex p Help the Aged* [1997] 3 FCR 573, Court of Appeal.

right to be consulted before a service is changed or withdrawn – for instance, when closing a care home, or making major changes to charges for non-residential community care services, or to the rules about eligibility for those services.[53] Occasionally, they may be about a *substantive* right to the service itself (with or without consultation); for instance, when a health authority broke an explicit promise to a disabled person about a 'home for life', and could not show an overriding reason for doing so.[54] Legislation in any case imposes additional, explicit obligations on NHS bodies to consult about changes to services.[55]

GIVING REASONS

For the most part in community care and NHS legislation, there is no explicit duty to give reasons for decisions. However, the courts sometimes demand reasons as evidence of the lawfulness of a decision. For instance, the Court of Appeal held it was unlawful for a local authority to place a 95-year-old woman in a nursing home without considering critically important factors or giving reasons.[56]

PERMISSION AND TIME LIMITS TO BRINGING A JUDICIAL REVIEW CASE

Permission is required from the High Court for a judicial review case to be brought.[57] Permission will be generally granted if the judge is satisfied that there is an arguable case. An application for judicial review must be brought promptly and in any event within three months from the date when the grounds of action arose.[58] For instance, when a local authority dithered too long in challenging the NHS about closure of local health services, the courts refused to allow the challenge to proceed.[59] Judicial review cases can take a considerable time (months or over a year) to come to court, although can be speeded up in particularly urgent cases.

Interim relief is also sometimes possible. For example, in one case the court ordered that services be provided until the dispute, about

---

53 *R(Chavda) v Harrow London Borough Council* [2007] EWHC 3064 Admin; also: *R(Carton) v Coventry City Council* (2001) 4 CCLR 41.

54 *R v North and East Devon Health Authority, ex p Coughlan* (1999) 2 CCLR 285, Court of Appeal.

55 *NHS Act 2006*, s.242, s.244 and SI 2002/3048. *Local Authority (Overview and Scrutiny Committees Health Scrutiny Functions) Regulations 2002*.

56 *R(Goldsmith) v Wandsworth London Borough Council* [2004] EWCA Civ 1170.

57 SI 1998/3132, r.54.4.

58 SI 1998/3132, r.54.5.

59 *R(Enfield London Borough Council) v Secretary of State for Health and Others* [2009] 743 Admin.

the withdrawal of night-sitter services from an elderly woman, was heard.[60]

WHO CAN BRING A JUDICIAL REVIEW CASE?

The claimant in a judicial review case must have a 'sufficient interest' in the case[61] – for example, service users or their carers. Sometimes established advisory organisations, representing particular groups of people, will also be recognised by the courts.[62]

WHETHER TO BRING A COMPLAINT OR A LEGAL CASE?

If the courts believe that there are appropriate 'alternative remedies', then they might insist that those remedies be used instead of judicial review. An obvious alternative remedy is the social services or NHS complaints procedure – as the Court of Appeal forcibly pointed out in cases about care home closures and adequacy of assessment of a person's needs.[63] However, the complaints procedure may be inappropriate if there is a clear legal issue at stake, or the alternative remedy would, for some reason, not be effective.[64]

---

60 *R v Staffordshire County Council, ex p Farley* [1997] 7 CL 572.

61 *Supreme Court Act 1981*, s.31.

62 *R v Sefton Metropolitan Borough Council, ex p Help the Aged* [1997] 3 FCR 573, Court of Appeal.

63 *R(Cowl) v Plymouth CC* [2001] EWCA Civ 1935; *R(Ireneschild) v Lambeth London Borough Council* [2007] EWCA Civ 234; *R(F) v Wirral Borough Council* [2009] EWHC 1626 Admin.

64 *R v Devon County Council, ex p Baker and Johns; R v Durham County Council, ex p Curtis and Brown* [1992] 158 LGRevR 241, Court of Appeal; *R v Sutton London Borough Council, ex p Tucker* [1998] CCLR 251; *R(Rodriguez-Bannister) v Somerset Partnership NHS and Social Care Trust* [2003] EWHC Admin 2184.

CHAPTER 4

Getting a community care assessment and getting services

- Duty to assess people who may be in need
  - Disabled people: right to an assessment
  - Health and housing services must be taken into account
  - Community care services
  - Who are community care services for?
- Screening people
  - People entitled to assessment even if they are unlikely to qualify for services
  - People entitled to assessment even if they have financial resources to pay
- Waiting for assessment
- Carrying out the assessment itself
  - Depth of assessment
  - Legal directions about assessment
- Assessing people in transition from child to adult
- Guidance: deaf-blind people, alcohol and drugs, learning disabilities
- Qualifying for services: fair access to care?
  - Setting rules about eligibility in line with available resources
  - Assessing risk to people's independence
  - Not excluding low-level services
  - Prevention
- Duty to meet need in the most cost-effective way
- Care plans

- Review and reassessment, reducing and withdrawing services
  - Closure of care homes
- Regulation and monitoring of care providers
  - Contracting out services: out of sight, out of mind?

SUMMARY

Community care revolves around s.47 of the NHS and Community Care Act 1990. This places a duty on local authorities to assess people's needs for community care services. These services are not contained in the 1990 Act but are scattered across five other pieces of legislation, which go back 60 years to the National Assistance Act 1948. This over-stretched legal framework is riddled with uncertainty and with the potential for shortcuts to be taken by local authorities (as described in Chapter 2).

PEOPLE IN NEED

Assessment is about deciding whether and what services should be provided for certain categories of person at least 18 years old. These categories are, in the main, older people, younger adults with disabilities (physical, sensory or learning), people with mental health needs, and people with drug or alcohol problems. However, not everybody in one of these categories and with a need gets a service. Local authorities apply 'eligibility criteria' as to who will qualify. They do this in order to restrict expenditure.

COMMUNITY CARE SERVICES

Services include provision of:

- residential accommodation with or without nursing care (i.e. care homes)

- personal care in people's own homes

- home help with household tasks

- respite care (giving people breaks from caring)

- holidays

- equipment to make life easier in people's homes (e.g. raised toilet seat, perching stool, special cutlery)

- adapting people's homes (e.g. grab rails, ramps, stairlifts)
- help with travel
- meals-on-wheels
- day centres
- recreational activities, and so on.

CARE PLANS
When local authorities have assessed a person, they must decide whether or not to arrange services for him or her. If they do so, they should produce a care plan that will indicate what the local authority has accepted to be its legal duty. Local authorities are meant to monitor and review people's care packages with reasonable attentiveness.

DUTY TO ASSESS PEOPLE WHO MAY BE IN NEED
Section 47 of the NHS and Community Care Act 1990 makes assessment a duty and a service in its own right. Assessment is the gateway to community care services; access to it is therefore crucial. In summary, the legislation states as follows. If it appears to a local authority that any person, for whom it may provide community care services, may have a need for such services, then the local authority must carry out an assessment. A request for assessment is not necessary. Having carried out the assessment, the local authority then has a duty to decide whether the person's needs call for services. In other words, if it is possible that a person might need community care services, then he or she is entitled to an assessment.

DISABLED PEOPLE: RIGHT TO AN ASSESSMENT
The legislation then states that if, during the assessment, it appears that the person is disabled then the authority must give special consideration as to what services are required under s.4 of the Disabled Persons (Services, Consultation and Representation) Act 1986. The 1986 Act, in turn, places a duty on the local authority to assess, on request by the disabled person or his or her carer, for services under the Chronically

Sick and Disabled Persons Act 1970.[1] This is long winded and confusing; it is so because central government failed to consolidate this legislation when the 1990 Act was passed. But, in sum, a local authority must assess a disabled person.

HEALTH AND HOUSING SERVICES MUST BE TAKEN INTO ACCOUNT

If the person being assessed might need health or housing services as well, social services must invite the local NHS primary care trust, health authority or housing authority to assist in the assessment – to such extent as is reasonable in the circumstances. Before deciding what services to provide, social services must take into account what the NHS or housing is likely to provide.[2]

COMMUNITY CARE SERVICES

It is a person's need for community care services that is being assessed under the NHS and Community Care Act 1990. To find out what these services are, one then has to go all round the houses because they are to be found in other legislation.[3]

Residential accommodation (usually, but not only, care homes) comes under s.21 of the National Assistance Act 1948 and s.117 of the Mental Health Act 1983. Non-residential services come under s.29 of the National Assistance Act 1948, s.2 of the Chronically Sick and Disabled Persons Act 1970, s.45 of the Health Services and Public Health Act 1968, schedule 20 of the NHS Act 2006 and s.117 of the Mental Health Act 1983.

WHO ARE COMMUNITY CARE SERVICES FOR?

Community care services are not available to just anyone. They are provided for certain groups of people defined in the legislation that lists the services. In summary, they are, broadly, people who are ill, physically disabled, mentally disordered in some way, who have a sensory impairment, who are elderly, or who have alcohol or drug problems.

---

1   *NHS and Community Care Act 1990*, s.47.
2   *NHS and Community Care Act 1990*, s.47.
3   *NHS and Community Care Act 1990*, s.46.

SCREENING PEOPLE

In order to determine who is eligible for an assessment, how quickly they should be assessed and what type of assessment they will get, local authorities operate screening procedures. Such screening is not legally prescribed, but in practice it acts as a potent filter; it has become associated with the shortcuts taken by local authorities (referred to in Chapter 2). It is sometimes used to avoid assessing people either at all or properly. Screening is increasingly carried out in telephone call centres.

The greater the shortcuts taken with screening (in terms of training, supervision, competence of staff, policies, procedures, etc.), the more chance there is of something going wrong.[4] The local government ombudsmen have emphasised the importance of adequate information-gathering at this screening stage, since, otherwise, local authorities are simply not in a position to make competent judgements about people's needs and priority for assessment.[5]

PEOPLE ENTITLED TO ASSESSMENT EVEN IF THEY ARE UNLIKELY TO QUALIFY FOR SERVICES

The courts have stated that there is a low threshold for access to assessment, which cannot be refused because of a lack of resources; either somebody is eligible for assessment, because of a possible community care need, or not. It is irrelevant that the person is unlikely to qualify for services under a local authority's eligibility rules, since assessment depends only on possible need for services and is anyway a benefit and duty in its own right.[6] This was established in a case involving a woman with anxiety and depression, who the local authority refused to assess.[7]

PEOPLE ENTITLED TO ASSESSMENT EVEN IF THEY HAVE FINANCIAL RESOURCES TO PAY

Statutory guidance has always stated that the 'assessment of financial means should ... follow the assessment of need and decisions about service provision'.[8] In practice, increasingly, local authorities attempt

---

4   See e.g. Commission for Social Care Inspection (2008) *Cutting the Cake Fairly.* London: CSCI, para 3.40.

5   E.g. *Stockport Metropolitan Borough Council 2003* (02/C/03831).

6   *R v Bristol City Council, ex p Penfold* [1998] 1 CCLR 315.

7   *R v Bristol City Council, ex p Penfold* [1998] 1 CCLR 315.

8   Department of Health (1990) *Community Care in the Next Decade and Beyond: Policy Guidance.* London: DH, para 3.31.

to minimise or even avoid this duty of assessment, by asking questions about people's finances first.[9]

WAITING FOR ASSESSMENT

A common shortcut taken by local authorities is to keep people waiting for assessment. Clearly, not everybody can be seen straightaway, but there is a history of excessive waiting times in community care. This has particularly affected occupational therapy services and the provision of daily living equipment and home adaptations.

The local government ombudsmen have investigated many cases of delay, stating that people must be assessed in a reasonable time; and a reasonable time in any particular case depends on the circumstances and urgency of the client's needs. Also:

(a) there should be well-defined criteria for assessing priorities

(b) the criteria should be applied after proper consideration and the person reassessed promptly in the light of any relevant new information, and

(c) people should be informed about the criteria, time-scales, their allocated priority, council services and reputable alternative suppliers.[10]

The length of waiting time should be in proportion to the urgency of need, but excessive waits even for people awarded low priority are not acceptable.[11] The same principles apply to waits for services, once assessment has taken place.

Local authorities sometimes console themselves by hitting imposed targets to assess people initially within 28 days of referral. However, if a so-called initial assessment is conducted quickly, but the real assessment is then delayed for many months, this will not save the local authority from a finding of maladministration by the local ombudsman.[12] Hitting targets on paper may be of little substantive value.

---

9 Dalley, G. (2008) (with Mandelstam, M.) *Assessment Denied? Council Responsibilities Towards Self-funders Moving into Care.* London: Relatives and Residents Association.

10 *Wakefield Metropolitan District Council 2004* (02/C/14023).

11 *Hackney London Borough Council 1992* (91/A/0482).

12 *Ealing London Borough Council 1999* (97/A/4069).

CARRYING OUT THE ASSESSMENT ITSELF

Great emphasis is placed on assessment in both legislation and in guidance. This emphasis is two-faced, like so many policies in community care (see Chapter 2). The good practice side is that people's needs should be properly assessed. The flip side is that organised assessment systems enable local authorities to ration services, drastically if need be, by separating out eligible from non-eligible people. To achieve this, local authorities have been given policy guidance from the Department of Health called 'fair access to care' (see below).

DEPTH OF ASSESSMENT

The law courts have stated that assessment should be proportionate to somebody's apparent needs,[13] and that local authorities should make reasonable efforts to ascertain what a person's needs are. But this does not extend to conducting the equivalent of a police CID (criminal investigation department) investigation.[14]

LEGAL DIRECTIONS ABOUT ASSESSMENT

The Department of Health has issued 'directions' about assessment. They amount to a duty. The local authority must:

(a) consult the person being assessed

(b) consider whether the person has any carers and, if appropriate, consult them, and

(c) take all reasonable steps to reach agreement – about the community care services to be provided – with both the person being assessed and, if appropriate, any carer.[15]

Apart from these directions, the Department has also issued policy guidance about assessment, under which local authorities have a duty to act.[16] In one case failure to take account properly of a person's preferences, as set out in this guidance, was unlawful;[17] likewise, when a local authority deviated from guidance about people's eligibility for services.[18]

---

13 *R v Bristol City Council, ex p Penfold* [1998] 1 CCLR 315.
14 *R v Kensington and Chelsea RB, ex p Kujtim* (1999) 2 CCLR 340, Court of Appeal.
15 Department of Health (2004) *Community Care Assessment Directions.* London: DH.
16 Department of Health (1990) *Community Care in the Next Decade and Beyond: Policy Guidance.* London: DH.
17 *R v North Yorkshire County Council, ex p Hargreaves* [1994] 26 BMLR 121.
18 *R(Heffernan) v Sheffield City Council* [2004] EWCH Admin 1377.

ASSESSING PEOPLE IN TRANSITION FROM CHILD TO ADULT

Specific legislation covers children or certain young people who have had statements of special educational needs – when they leave school or further or higher education institutions. It confers duties of communication, referral and assessment on education authorities, social services authorities, further or higher education institutions and the Learning and Skills Council.[19]

More generally, the transition of children to adult services (at age 18) has long been identified as a problem. For instance, the local ombudsmen have found maladministration when there is a lack of advance planning, followed by sometimes belated assessment and provision of community care services.[20]

GUIDANCE: DEAF-BLIND PEOPLE, ALCOHOL AND DRUGS, LEARNING DISABILITIES

Department of Health guidance states that local authorities should keep a record of deaf-blind people locally. They should also ensure that:

(a) assessments are carried out by a specially trained person in relation to the need for one-to-one human contact, assistive technology and rehabilitation

(b) services are appropriate

(c) trained one-to-one support workers are provided where the need has been assessed

(d) information about services is accessible

(e) a senior manager has responsibility for services for deaf-blind people.[21]

Other guidance states that local authorities should attach a high priority to misusers of drugs and alcohol, that eligibility criteria must be sensitive to people's needs, that assessment procedures must be adequate and expert (perhaps by making use of the independent sector), etc.[22]

Further guidance still sets out various matters including that people with learning disabilities should be treated as individuals, parents and carers should be fully involved in decisions about services, and that

19 Disabled Persons (Services, Consultation and Representation) Act 1986, s.5.
20 E.g. Liverpool City Council 1997 (96/C/0581).
21 LAC(2009)6. Department of Health. Social Care for Deafblind Children and Adults. London: DH.
22 LAC(93)2. Department of Health. Alcohol and Drug Services Within Community Care. London: DH.

local authorities should give assurances (especially to ageing parents) about meeting people's needs on a lifelong basis.[23]

QUALIFYING FOR SERVICES: FAIR ACCESS TO CARE?

The courts have confirmed that when local authorities set rules about eligibility, they may take account of resources. They have also held that once a person is assessed as coming over a locally set rule or threshold, then his or her need must be met; a lack of resources is no legal excuse for failure to do this.[24]

Authorities can alter the threshold from time to time, although they must consult about this.[25] Consequently, people's right to services can fluctuate not just according to their own changing needs and circumstances, but according to a changeable local policy. Since 2003, local authorities have applied a system of eligibility called 'fair access to care' in line with Department of Health guidance.[26] Its title is something of a misnomer and belies the use to which it has been put. Due for revision in 2010,[27] this system reflects the rules stipulated about eligibility by the courts, and has been used across England to drive thresholds upward and make them more difficult to cross. Thus in 2007, 25 per cent fewer households were being assisted than in 1997; and the Commission for Social Care Inspection warned of the consequent threat to people's dignity, welfare, quality of life and physical safety.[28]

SETTING RULES ABOUT ELIGIBILITY IN LINE WITH AVAILABLE RESOURCES

Local authorities have to set thresholds of eligibility realistically, because otherwise too many people would qualify for help in relation to available resources. This would be a legal problem, because of the rule that once an individual is assessed as having eligible needs, those needs must be met[29] – even if, for example, it costs £3700 per week

---

23 LAC(92)15. Department of Health. *Social Care for Adults with Learning Disabilities (Mental Handicap)*. London: DH.

24 *R v Gloucestershire County Council, ex p Barry* [1997] 2 All ER 1, House of Lords.

25 LAC(2002)13. Department of Health. *Fair Access to Care Services: Guidance on Eligibility Criteria for Adult Social Care.* London: DH, para 20; *R(Chavda) v Harrow London Borough Council* [2007] EWHC 3064 Admin.

26 LAC(2002)13. Department of Health. *Fair access …*

27 Department of Health (2009) *Prioritising Need in the Context of Putting People First: A Whole System Approach to Eligibility for Care.* London: DH.

28 Henwood, M. and Hudson, B. (2008) *Lost to the System? The Impact of Fair Access to Care.* London: Commission for Social Care Inspection. Also: Commission for Social Care Inspection (2008) *The State of Social Care in England 2006–07.* London: CSCI.

29 *R v Gloucestershire County Council, ex p Barry* [1997] 2 All ER 1, House of Lords.

to cover a specialist placement for a person with learning disabilities, autism and epilepsy.[30]

However, wherever the threshold is set, political honesty is required. A high threshold may seem mean and be politically unpopular. Yet a generous threshold requires a correspondingly generous allocation of resources; without this a mismatch arises between the duty owed to people and the resources available to perform it. Local authorities then execute shortcuts that run the risk of being unlawful.

For instance, in practice some authorities informally reset the previously agreed and publicised threshold of eligibility in order to relieve the pressure on an inadequate budget. This is maladministration[31] and potentially unlawful. Others might – irrespective of a person's assessed, eligible needs – begin to apply impermissible blanket policies in terms of what services they will or won't provide,[32] or impose rigid cost ceilings on care provision for individual service users.[33] Alternatively, they may keep people waiting for services for inordinate periods of time, or meet only a proportion of a person's assessed eligible need.[34] Such shortcuts risk findings of unlawfulness by the law courts or of maladministration by the local government ombudsmen; yet they are widespread.

ASSESSING RISK TO PEOPLE'S INDEPENDENCE

The fair access to care guidance from the Department of Health sets out four different levels of risk to a person's independence: critical, substantial, moderate and low. Each authority must then set and apply its local eligibility threshold.[35]

In practice, a majority of local authorities state that they will meet needs at a critical or substantial level, but not at moderate or low. A very few will meet critical needs only. Others, apparently more generous, will meet moderate needs as well as critical and substantial. A few will also meet low needs. Department of Health guidance has approved use of a critical threshold only, when a local authority believes it necessary.[36] As long as, in any one individual case, human rights are not breached and

30   *R(Alloway) v Bromley London Borough Council* [2004] EWHC 2108 (Admin).
31   Local ombudsman investigation: *Cambridgeshire County Council 2001* (99/B/04621).
32   Local ombudsman investigation: *Salford City Council 2003* (01/C/17519).
33   *R(Alloway) v Bromley London Borough Council* [2004] EWHC 2108 (Admin).
34   *R v Islington London Borough Council, ex p Rixon* [1997] 1 ELR 477.
35   LAC(2002)13. Department of Health. *Fair access …*
36   Department of Health (2003) *Fair Access to Care Services: Practice Guidance*. London: DH.

other legal obligations are complied with, there would appear to be no overwhelming legal obstacle to such a strict approach.[37]

The guidance sets out indicators of what constitutes critical, substantial, moderate or low risk to a person's independence. It is noteworthy that even under the critical category, these indicators are not confined to matters of life and limb. However, in practice some local authorities seem to overlook this, perhaps particularly in the case of older people. The indicators are as follows:

(a) Critical risk to independence

- Life is, or will be, threatened; and/or

- significant health problems have developed or will develop; and/or

- there is, or will be, little or no choice and control over vital aspects of the immediate environment; and/or

- serious abuse or neglect has occurred or will occur; and/or

- there is, or will be, an inability to carry out vital personal care or domestic routines; and/or

- vital involvement in work, education or learning cannot or will not be sustained; and/or

- vital social support systems and relationships cannot or will not be sustained; and/or

- vital family and other social roles and responsibilities cannot or will not be undertaken.

(b) Substantial risk to independence

- There is, or will be, only partial choice and control over the immediate environment; and/or

- abuse or neglect has occurred or will occur; and/or

- there is, or will be, an inability to carry out the majority of personal care or domestic routines; and/or

---

37 *R(Chavda) v Harrow London Borough Council* [2007] EWHC 3064 Admin; *R v East Sussex County Council, ex p Tandy* [1998] 2 All ER 769, House of Lords.

- involvement in many aspects of work, education or learning cannot or will not be sustained; and/or

- the majority of social support systems and relationships cannot or will not be sustained; and/or

- the majority of family and other social roles and responsibilities cannot or will not be undertaken.

(c) Moderate risk to independence

- There is, or will be, an inability to carry out several personal care or domestic routines; and/or

- involvement in several aspects of work, education or learning cannot or will not be sustained; and/or

- several social support systems and relationships cannot or will not be sustained; and/or

- several family and other social roles and responsibilities cannot or will not be undertaken.

(d) Low risk to independence

- There is, or will be, an inability to carry out one or two personal care or domestic routines; and/or

- involvement in one or two aspects of work, education or learning cannot or will not be sustained; and/or

- one or two social support systems and relationships cannot or will not be sustained; and/or

- one or two family and other social roles and responsibilities cannot or will not be undertaken.[38]

NOT EXCLUDING LOW-LEVEL SERVICES

The guidance envisages that rationing decisions will be based on the level of a person's need. Accordingly it states that local authorities should not have blanket policies to exclude specific services.[39] This is because there is not a straightforward equation between a low level of service and a low level of need.

---

38 LAC(2003)13. Department of Health. *Fair Access* ... para 16.
39 LAC(2002)13. Department of Health. *Fair Access* ... para 23.

Despite this, many local authorities fall into the trap of rationing by type of service rather than by level of need. This may lead them into trouble; for instance, the local government ombudsman has found maladministration because of the refusal of local authorities to contemplate apparently low-level services such as cleaning – for a man who was a wheelchair user, diabetic, doubly incontinent and an amputee.[40] Similarly the local ombudsman and health service ombudsman jointly investigated, and criticised, the failure to provide for the shopping needs (one hour a week) of a man with mental health problems – who suffered from agoraphobia, social phobia and whose grandmother, his mainstay, had just died.[41]

The Commission for Social Care Inspection has criticised heavily the exclusion of such 'low level' services by local authorities.[42]

PREVENTION

The fair access to care guidance states that prevention should be built into a local authority's eligibility scheme.[43] Draft replacement guidance emphasises still further the importance of prevention, and suggests that excessively strict eligibility criteria are counter-productive if they lead to a longer term rise in serious need.[44]

DUTY TO MEET NEED IN THE MOST COST-EFFECTIVE WAY

Once a local authority has set its threshold of eligibility for a period of time, then it has a duty to meet a person's needs if they are assessed as coming over that threshold. This is an absolute duty and a lack of resources is no defence for non-performance.[45] Clearly, for service users this is a potent legal rule; for managers whose budget is at breaking point, it is a nightmare.

However, if there is more than one option available, then the local authority is obliged to offer only the cheapest. But that option must genuinely be capable of meeting the assessed, eligible needs. In relation to cost-effectiveness, the courts have noted that there is nothing generous, legally, about community care. For instance, placing somebody in a care

---

40 *Westminster County Council 1996* (93/A/4250).

41 *Middlesbrough Council and Tees, Esk and Wear Valleys NHS Trust 2008* (O6/C/10526 and JW-11585).

42 Commission for Social Care Inspection (2008) *The State of Social Care in England 2006–07*. London: CSCI.

43 LAC(2002)13. Department of Health. *Fair Access ...* para 22.

44 Department of Health (2009) *Prioritising Need in the Context of Putting People First: A Whole System Approach to Eligibility for Social Care*. London: DH, para 27.

45 *R v Gloucestershire County Council, ex p Barry* [1997] 2 All ER 1, House of Lords.

home may be cheaper than supporting him or her at home.[46] Likewise using a commode rather than a stairlift for night-time toilet needs[47] – or leaving a person (who was not incontinent) in incontinence pads all night, rather than providing a night-time visit to help her on to the commode, was held to be lawful.[48] Nonetheless, if the only practical option is more expensive than the local authority would normally contemplate, it must still spend the money and meet the need.[49]

CARE PLANS

Care plans may not be mentioned in legislation but legally they are pivotal. Department of Health guidance states that, following a decision about the services to be provided, a care plan should be drawn up by the local authority. The plan should contain details about objectives, services, agencies to be involved, costs, needs that cannot be met, date of first review, and so on.[50] The form and complexity of a care plan will vary depending on the level and type of service involved. The law courts have held that:

(a) either a failure to follow, or at least to have proper regard to, this guidance may be unlawful

(b) a care plan is evidence of what a local authority has accepted as its duty to meet a person's needs, and

(c) failure to adhere to the care plan is likely to indicate breach of duty.[51]

REVIEW AND REASSESSMENT, REDUCING AND WITHDRAWING SERVICES

Reassessment is a legal prerequisite to any substantial change, reduction or withdrawal of services. Guidance states that review and reassessment should, other than exceptionally, be face to face, be conducted directly

---

46 *R v Lancashire County Council, ex p RADAR* [1996] 4 All ER 422, Court of Appeal.

47 *R v Sheffield City Council, ex p Low* (2000) unreported, Court of Appeal (renewed application for permission to bring judicial review case).

48 *R(McDonald) v Kensington and Chelsea Royal London Borough* [2009] EWHC 1582 Admin (permission to apply for judicial review refused). Also: *R(Heffernan) v Sheffield City Council* [2004] EWCH Admin 1377.

49 *R(Alloway) v Bromley London Borough Council* [2004] EWHC 2108 (Admin).

50 Department of Health (1990) *Community Care in the Next Decade and Beyond: Policy Guidance.* London: DH, para 3.24. Social Services Inspectorate; Social Work Services Group (1991) *Care Management and Assessment: Practitioners' Guide.* London/Edinburgh: Department of Health, Scottish Office, para 4.37. Also: LAC(2002)13. Department of Health. *Fair Access ...* para 47. Also: Department of Health (2001) *Guidance on the Single Assessment Process for Older People.* London: DH, Annex E.

51 *R v Islington London Borough Council, ex p Rixon* [1997] 1 ELR 477.

by the local authority and not by service providers, and be carried out by a competent professional.[52] This guidance is by no means always adhered to. The local ombudsman has pointed out with some restraint the maladministration involved when a manager instructed staff to review on the telephone, a deaf person with learning disabilities.[53]

Substantial change to services is generally lawful if the reassessment reveals that (a) a person's needs have reduced or changed, (b) those needs can reasonably be met in another way, or (c) the threshold of eligibility has changed (so that the person, though with the same needs, no longer qualifies for assistance). Absent these and the withdrawal may be unlawful – as the courts found when a local authority tried to halve the care of a woman with multiple sclerosis in order to contain expenditure.[54] However, local authorities can also withhold services in the face of unreasonable behaviour by service users, although there are specific provisos to this – in particular, where the unreasonable behaviour is linked, for example, to a mental disorder of some description.[55] Guidance on fair access to care warns against over precipitate withdrawal of services from people, when a local authority has changed and made stricter its eligibility rules.[56]

Local authorities sometimes conduct reviews more intensively when the overall purpose is not just to check that needs are being met adequately, but also to reduce or withdraw services in order to save money.

CLOSURE OF CARE HOMES

A significant number of legal cases have involved challenges to local authority decisions to close care homes (maybe all their care homes)[57] and transfer residents elsewhere. As long as the local authority has consulted satisfactorily and taken account of relevant issues, such cases generally fail, even when argued on human rights grounds. The courts have tended to accept evidence that it is the way in which people are

---

52 LAC(2002)13. Department of Health. *Fair Access* ... paras 60–68.
53 *Birmingham City Council 2008* (05/C/18474).
54 *R v Birmingham City Council, ex p Killigrew* (2000) 3 CCLR 109.
55 *R v Kensington and Chelsea RB, ex p Kujtim* (1999) 2 CCLR 340, Court of Appeal.
56 LAC(2002)13. Department of Health. *Fair Access* ... paras 60–68.
57 *R v Wandsworth London Borough Council, ex p Beckwith* [1996] 1 FCR 504, House of Lords.

moved to another home, rather than the principle of a move itself, that is important;[58] likewise, if day centres are being closed.[59]

REGULATION AND MONITORING OF CARE PROVIDERS

Registration and inspection of care providers (both the independent sector and local authorities) have been under the Care Standards Act 2000 and were the responsibility of the Commission for Social Care Inspection (CSCI) until the end of March 2009.

From April 2009, a new Care Quality Commission (CQC) was formed, replacing the CSCI, the Healthcare Commission and the Mental Health Act Commission. This is under the Health and Social Care Act 2008; new sets of care standards are being developed under the 2008 Act and will replace those under the 2000 Act. The Commission can issue statutory warning notices, impose, vary or remove registration conditions, issue financial penalty notices, suspend or cancel registration, prosecute specified offences and issue simple cautions.[60]

CONTRACTING OUT SERVICES: OUT OF SIGHT, OUT OF MIND?

Local authorities increasingly contract out services to the independent sector, against a background of financial and performance targets imposing great pressure on both commissioners and providers to pare down costs and cut corners. This can erode standards of care.

The regulatory legislation is, in principle, therefore more important than ever. However, regulatory bodies do not always detect or prevent poor, and even calamitous, practices. This means that local authorities should take even more seriously their responsibility to monitor their own and contracted-out services and to sort out problems. The local government ombudsman has been highly critical of local authorities that have failed to do this, with vulnerable people then suffering harm and even death – for example, when staff from a domiciliary care agency have foreseeably failed to turn up to visit an elderly, highly vulnerable person.[61]

---

58 E.g. *R(Wilson) v Coventry City Council* [2008] EWHC 2300 Admin; *R(Cowl) v Plymouth CC* [2001] EWCA Civ 1935; *R(Dudley) v East Sussex County Council* [2003] EWHC Admin 1093; *R(Haggerty) v St Helens Metropolitan Borough Council* [2003] EWHC Admin 803.
59 *R(Bishop) v Bromley London Borough Council* [2006] EWHC 2148 Admin.
60 Care Quality Commission (2009) *Enforcement Policy.* London: CQC.
61 *Sheffield City Council 2007* (05/C/06420).

CHAPTER 5

Community care
services: care homes

- Care homes: different funding and charging arrangements
- Basic rules for placing people in care homes
- What is residential accommodation?
- When a local authority must, or may, provide residential accommodation
  - Duty to provide residential accommodation
  - Strength of duty to provide residential accommodation
  - Power to provide residential accommodation
- Choice of residential accommodation
  - Choice and cost of care home
  - Local authority duty to pay higher costs to meet a person's assessed need
  - Local authorities must give people genuine choice and information
  - Topping up of care home fees by families
  - Topping up must involve choice to be lawful
  - Local authorities turning a blind eye to top-up fees demanded by care homes
- Transparency about care home fees
  - Information about increase in fees and NHS-funded nursing care
- Paying for residential accommodation
  - Overall duty to charge
  - Personal expenses allowance
  - Temporary residents
  - Less-dependent residents
  - Assessment of couples
  - Assessing a person's capital assets
  - Whose capital asset is it?

49

- Disregarding capital in the means test: rules about personal injury compensation
- Award of personal injury damages
- Disregarding a person's home for 12 weeks
- Disregarding the person's home if other people are living in it
- Legal and beneficial owners of property
- Deferring payment for care
- Notional capital
- Giving assets away to avoid paying care home charges
- Practicalities of demanding notional capital
- Assessment of income
- Taking account of income
- Disregarding income: personal injury compensation
- Pursuit of debt
- Pursuing payment from a third party
- Placing a legal land charge on the property for money owing
- Insolvency proceedings

SUMMARY

Local authorities place people in residential accommodation (typically care homes) under s.21 of the National Assistance Act 1948. Depending on what sort of needs people have, and what type of home they need to go to, local authorities set a 'usual cost level'. This indicates the maximum amount they are generally prepared to pay. There are then rules about giving people a choice of care home and about the 'topping up' of care home fees (typically by family), so that people can go to more expensive care homes. There are further (in part, absurdly complicated) rules about how people should be charged. Local authorities and care homes do not always seem to know what these rules are, let alone stick to them; this is yet another example of the shortcuts referred to in Chapter 2. It seems particularly unfortunate that the rules are so complex, misunderstood and misapplied, given the sums of money involved in care home fees and the vulnerability of those within the care homes. The courts themselves have characterised some of these rules as complex, labyrinthine, unclear and inaccessible.[1]

---

1   *Crofton v NHS Litigation Authority* [2007] EWCA Civ 71.

CARE HOMES: DIFFERENT FUNDING AND CHARGING ARRANGEMENTS

Many people are placed in care homes under s.21 of the National Assistance Act 1948; this chapter deals with the rules.

However, people can end up in care homes in other ways. If a resident is deemed by the NHS to have 'continuing health care' status, then the NHS should fund the accommodation, board, personal care and nursing care – all of which will then be free of charge to the resident under the NHS Act 2006 (see Chapter 14). In addition, a person may be placed, free of charge, in residential accommodation by way of aftercare under s.117 of the Mental Health Act 1983 (see Chapter 6).

Alternatively, people might be self-funding, in which case they have their own contract with the care home. People might be in this position when they have been assessed by a local authority as having resources over the relevant financial threshold, and as having the mental and physical ability (albeit with assistance) to make their own arrangements. Other people might simply decide to make their own arrangements anyway, without having had a local authority assessment; this might be because they don't want one or because the authority has declined, perhaps unlawfully, to give them one.[2]

BASIC RULES FOR PLACING PEOPLE IN RESIDENTIAL ACCOMMODATION

Local authorities place people in council-owned care homes (where they still exist) or in independent care homes.[3] The person must be at least 18 years old and have a need for care and attention. This need must arise from age, illness, disability or any other circumstances. The care and attention required must not be available other than by the provision of accommodation under s.21 of the Act. The courts have added (particularly where the accommodation is not going to be in the form of a care home) that such care and attention must involve an element of 'looking after'. This means personal care, help with household tasks, help with shopping – but a need for health services doesn't count. The emphasis is on present need, but the local authority could intervene to prevent a lesser need getting substantially worse.[4]

---

2   Dalley, G. (with Mandelstam, M.) (2008) *Assessment Denied? Council Responsibilities Towards Self-funders Moving into Care.* London: Relatives and Residents Association.

3   *National Assistance Act 1948*, ss.21, 26.

4   *R(M) v Slough Borough Council* [2008] UKHL 52.

In deciding whether somebody really needs care and attention not otherwise available, local authorities are allowed to take into account a person's financial resources. However, they must ignore the person's capital resources (savings, value of their home, etc.) under a certain level (£23,000 at the time of writing). But this does not mean that if people have more than that sum, they will always be left to make their own arrangements. For instance, they might lack the mental and physical ability to make their own arrangements and not have family assistance, no matter how much money they have. In which case, the local authority must make the arrangements but then charge the person the full cost.[5]

WHAT IS RESIDENTIAL ACCOMMODATION?

Residential accommodation under s.21 of the National Assistance Act 1948 is often taken to refer to care homes only. However, it can apply also to hostels, hotels, bed and breakfast accommodation and, sometimes, ordinary housing. Thus, where a person's community care needs cannot be met in any other way except through provision of ordinary housing, the courts have held that a duty to arrange such housing can arise under s.21.[6] This would tend to be the exception rather than the rule, though.[7]

Local authorities can place people in care homes with or without nursing, that is, residential homes or nursing homes. If they place a person in a nursing home, they must first gain consent from the local NHS primary care trust.[8] The NHS is responsible for paying for 'funded nursing care' in a nursing home, amounting to £106.30 per week (see Chapter 13).

WHEN A LOCAL AUTHORITY MUST, OR MAY, PROVIDE RESIDENTIAL ACCOMMODATION

Under s.21 of the National Assistance Act 1948, local authorities have both duties and powers.

DUTY TO PROVIDE RESIDENTIAL ACCOMMODATION

An overall duty applies to people who are ordinarily resident within the area of the local authority (or who are in urgent need) – and are in

---

5 LAC(98)19. Department of Health. *Community Care (Residential Accommodation) Act 1998.* London: DH, paras 10–11.

6 *R(Bernard) v Enfield London Borough Council* [2002] EWHC Admin 2282.

7 *R(Wahid) v Tower Hamlets London Borough Council* [2002] EWCA Civ 287.

8 *National Assistance Act 1948*, s.26(1C).

need of care and attention not otherwise available to them, by reason of age, illness, disability or any other circumstances. (Ordinary residence is explained in Chapter 11.)

More specifically, local authorities must also arrange residential accommodation (a) temporarily for people in urgent and unforeseen need of it, and (b) for people with a mental disorder who are either ordinarily resident within the local authority or in the area of the authority but of no settled residence.[9]

STRENGTH OF DUTY TO PROVIDE RESIDENTIAL ACCOMMODATION
When a duty arises because a person is assessed to need residential accommodation, the courts have accepted that the duty is more or less absolute in the sense that it must be met irrespective of resources.[10]

POWER TO PROVIDE RESIDENTIAL ACCOMMODATION
In addition to duties, there are also powers to arrange residential accommodation for other groups of people. These are:

(a) people of no settled residence

(b) people ordinarily resident in another local authority (and with the consent of the other authority)

(c) people with a mental disorder ordinarily resident in the area of another authority but who have become resident in the authority's area following discharge from hospital

(d) in relation to the prevention of illness, the care of those who are ill, or their aftercare

(e) specifically people who are dependent on drugs or alcohol

(f) expectant and nursing mothers, in particular the provision of mother and baby homes.[11]

CHOICE OF RESIDENTIAL ACCOMMODATION
The Department of Health has passed directions (creating a duty) and guidance, giving people the right to choose what care home they go to. There is also the option of the family or somebody else 'topping up'

---

9   LAC(93)10. Department of Health. *Approvals and Directions for Arrangements From 1st April 2003 Made Under Schedule 8 to the NHS Act 1977 and Sections 21 and 29 of the National Assistance Act 1948.* London: DH, Appendix 1.
10   *R v Sefton Metropolitan Borough Council, ex p Help the Aged* [1997] 3 FCR 392; [1997] 3 FCR 573, Court of Appeal.
11   LAC(93)10. Department of Health. *Approvals and Directions ...* Appendix 1.

the fee. This enables a person to go to the home of their choice, even if it costs more than the local authority is legally obliged to pay. The rules are, in principle, quite simple; the practice not so. There appears to be significant flouting of the rules by both local authorities and care homes. This is to be deplored, given how important the decision to enter a care home is, together with the vulnerability of the resident, the anxiety and concern of the family, the location, the character, the standards of care – and the amounts of money involved.

CHOICE AND COST OF CARE HOME
The directions create a duty. They state that a local authority should arrange residential accommodation of a person's choice – if the following conditions are satisfied. The person must have an assessed, eligible need. The preferred accommodation must be suitable for the person's needs and also be available. The cost of the placement must come within the usual cost level specified by the local authority for the type of need and accommodation. However, crucially, the directions do not dilute the local authority's duty to arrange the person's preferred accommodation – even at a higher than usual cost – if the assessed need demands it.[12]

LOCAL AUTHORITY DUTY TO PAY HIGHER COSTS TO MEET A PERSON'S ASSESSED NEED
Department of Health guidance illustrates why a local authority might have to pay more than usual, in order to meet a person's assessed needs. For instance, some residents might have high levels of need, and require special diets or additional facilities for medical or cultural reasons. Likewise, a person might be assessed as needing to be in a particular geographical area (e.g. to be near relatives), where the costs of the placement exceed the local authority's usual cost level.[13]

LOCAL AUTHORITIES MUST GIVE PEOPLE GENUINE CHOICE AND INFORMATION
Department of Health guidance states that the choice of care home should not be illusory. Local authorities should give people information

---

12 LAC(92)27. Department of Health. *National Assistance Act 1948 (Choice of Accommodation) Directions 1992.* London: DH.

13 LAC(2004)20. Department of Health. *Guidance on National Assistance Act 1948 (Choice of Accommodation) Directions 1992.* London: DH, para 2.5.

so they can exercise real choice; encourage the presence of a relative, carer or advocate; and keep a written record of the conversation, decisions taken and preferences expressed.[14] Guidance warns against arbitrary setting of a usual cost level;[15] but in practice, as the local ombudsman has found, local authorities may set the level so low as to deprive people of reasonable – or even of all – choice.[16]

TOPPING UP OF CARE HOME FEES BY FAMILIES

Linked to the principle of basic choice is another, that of 'topping up'. This allows the resident, over and beyond exercising a reasonable choice of which care home to enter, to live in a more expensive one – that is, more expensive than the local authority believes is necessary in order to meet the assessed needs of the person.

For this to happen, a third party (not the resident) must be willing to pay the difference between the usual cost level set by the local authority and the actual fee charged by the care home. Regulations allow for this to happen. The resident himself or herself can 'self top up' but only (a) during the first 12 weeks of the stay (when a financial disregard of a person's property must be applied), or (b) in the case of a 'deferred payment agreement' (see below). The local authority is under a duty to accept top-up arrangements by a third party, but only if that third party can reasonably be expected to make the payments for the whole period in question.[17] In case of default by the third party, the local authority remains liable for the fee owing to the care home.[18]

TOPPING UP MUST INVOLVE CHOICE TO BE LAWFUL

Topping up is lawful only if there is a choice involved in going to the more expensive care home. This means there must also be a cheaper care home, capable of meeting the person's needs, and charging fees within the local authority's usual cost level. If, however, no such cheaper home is available that would meet the assessed needs, then, clearly, entering the more expensive home is not through choice. In which case, the local

---

14 LAC(2004)20. Department of Health. *Guidance* ... para 7.2.
15 LAC(2004)20. Department of Health. *Guidance* ... para 2.5.7.
16 *Merton London Borough Council 1999* (97/A/3218).
17 SI 2001/3441. *National Assistance (Residential Accommodation) (Additional Payments and Assessment of Resources) (Amendment) (England) Regulations 2001.* See: *R(Daniel) v Leeds City Council* [2004] EWHC 562.
18 LAC(2004)20. Department of Health. *Guidance* ... para 3.5.2.

authority should itself cover the greater expense, and a top-up should not be demanded or paid.[19]

In principle, therefore, the rules about topping up are surprisingly simple. In practice, it seems they are broken frequently by local authorities, who too often seem reluctant to explain to families what the rules really are.[20]

LOCAL AUTHORITIES TURNING A BLIND EYE TO TOP-UP FEES DEMANDED BY CARE HOMES

Even when there is no choice involved, some local authorities do not request a top-up themselves, but leave it up to the care home to try to extract such a contribution from the family. The local authority then turns a blind eye.[21] This, too, is unlawful, since the local authority is responsible ultimately for the whole fee. Department of Health guidance stresses that councils 'must never encourage or otherwise imply that care home providers can or should seek further contributions from individuals in order to meet assessed needs'.[22]

TRANSPARENCY ABOUT CARE HOME FEES

The care home market is characterised by a lack of contractual transparency about just what is being paid for, whether by self-funding residents or by local authorities.[23] Given the high level of care home fees, this is both extraordinary and concerning – and even suggests exploitation. It is therefore worth spelling out some of the detail.

Regulations stipulate that the care home must provide a range of information in a service user's guide. This should include:

(a) description of standard services offered

(b) terms and conditions relating to the provision of the accommodation, including food, personal care and nursing care

(c) details of the total fee payable for these

(d) arrangements for charging for additional services

19 LAC(2004)20. Department of Health. *Guidance* ... para 2.5.5.
20 Continuing Care Conference (2007) *Paying for Care: Third Party Top-ups and Cross-subsidies.* London: CCC.
21 Continuing Care Conference (2007) *Paying for Care* ... p.4.
22 LAC(2004)20. Department of Health. *Guidance* ... paras 4.4–4.5.
23 Office of Fair Trading (2005) *Care Homes for Older People in the UK.* London: OFT.

(e) a statement as to whether charges vary if the person is not funding themselves (e.g. the local authority is paying)

(f) a standard form of contract

(g) the most recent inspection report

(h) a summary of the complaints procedure.

In addition, specific information must be given to each person, on the day he or she becomes a resident, setting out: the fees payable for the accommodation (including food) and for the nursing and personal care (and, except where a single fee is payable, the services to which each fee relates), and the method of payment.[24]

INFORMATION ABOUT INCREASE IN FEES AND NHS-FUNDED NURSING CARE

The home must inform the service user of any increase in fees, together with reasons for the increase, or of variation in the method of payment. This has to be done, if practicable, at least one month in advance, or otherwise as soon as practicable.

In nursing homes, the person must be informed whether a nursing contribution from the NHS is payable (see Chapter 13). If it is paid, the home has to give the service user a statement specifying the date of the payment and the amount of the nursing contribution and either (a) the date on which the care home will pay the amount of the nursing contribution to the service user or deduct the amount from the fees, or (b) if the nursing contribution is not to be so paid or deducted, whether and how it is taken into account in calculating the fees.

These rules do not apply where the NHS primary care trust – as opposed to the local authority – has actually arranged for the provision of accommodation itself.[25]

PAYING FOR RESIDENTIAL ACCOMMODATION

If a local authority places a person in residential accommodation under s.21 of the National Assistance Act 1948, it has a duty to apply a detailed test of resources in order to decide what the resident should pay. This is in contrast to non-residential services, for which local authorities are not obliged to charge (although they exercise fully the discretion to do

---

24   SI 2001/3965. *Care Homes Regulations 2001*, r.5.
25   SI 2001/3965. *Care Homes Regulations 2001*, rr.5–5A.

so in practice). It should not be assumed that local authority staff are always conversant with, or apply, the rules; so it is worth spelling out some of the detail, albeit simplified.

Note. It should be stressed that the rules are in places excessively complicated – for example, the rules about personal injury compensation payments. Reference should be made to the National Assistance Act 1948, the National Assistance (Assessment of Resources) Regulations 1992 (SI 1992/2977), and the Charging for Residential Accommodation Guide, a loose-leaf, regularly updated manual of guidance available from the Department of Health. The regulations frequently cross-refer to, and rely on, the Income Support (General) Regulations 1987 (SI 1987/1967).

OVERALL DUTY TO CHARGE

Generally speaking, local authorities have a duty to apply a test of resources. In deciding whether a person needs residential accommodation – that is, whether the person needs care and attention not otherwise available – the local authority must disregard (i.e. ignore) the person's resources up to (for 2009–10) £23,000.

If the authority is providing the accommodation directly, then the charge should be at a standard rate and represent the full cost to the local authority of provision. However, if the authority is satisfied that a person cannot afford to pay this, then it must charge less. In the case of independent care providers, the charging procedure is more or less the same: the local authority pays the provider for the cost of the place, and the resident repays the authority the amount he or she has been assessed to pay.[26]

PERSONAL EXPENSES ALLOWANCE

In calculating the weekly amount payable by a resident, the authority must assume that he or she will require a certain amount of money for personal requirements. This is called the personal expenses allowance and is currently (2009–10) set at £21.90 per week.[27] Department of Health guidance states that its purpose is to allow residents to have money to spend as they wish, and that it should not be spent on services that have been contracted for, or that have been assessed by the local authority or the NHS as necessary to meet a person's needs.[28]

---

26 See: *National Assistance Act 1948*, ss.22, 26. And: SI 1992/2977. *National Assistance (Assessment of Resources) Regulations 1992*, r.20.

27 *National Assistance Act 1948*, s.22. And: SI 2003/628. *National Assistance (Sums for Personal Requirements) (England) Regulations 2003*.

28 Department of Health (2009) *Charging for Residential Accommodation Guidance.* London: DH, para 5.001.

The amount allocated by the regulations is arguably inadequate.[29] There is also evidence that care homes misuse people's personal allowances, by pooling them and spending them collectively.[30] In one instance, a person's allowance in a local authority care home was put into a general 'extras account' to pay for newspapers (which she could not read), piano tuning, aquarium maintenance and plants. The local ombudsman found maladministration.[31]

TEMPORARY RESIDENTS

A temporary resident is a person whose stay is unlikely to exceed 52 weeks or, in exceptional circumstances, is unlikely substantially to exceed 52 weeks.[32] For the first eight weeks of such a temporary stay, the local authority has discretion to limit what it charges. In other words, it is not obliged to follow the statutory test of resources in these circumstances although it can do so.[33] This gives local authorities considerable discretion in deciding what to charge for respite care or short-term breaks.

Beyond a stay of eight weeks the local authority is obliged to apply the statutory charging procedure. However, the special rules applying to temporary residents mean that a local authority must disregard certain assets – for instance, the person's own home (when he or she is intending to return there, or is taking steps to sell it and acquire another more suitable) – and certain housing-related costs and home commitments, attendance allowance and disability allowance.[34]

Guidance explains that if a stay, thought to be permanent, turns out to be temporary only, then it would be 'unreasonable' for the authority to continue to apply the permanent residence rules to the resident. Conversely, if what was expected originally to be a temporary stay turns out to be permanent, the permanent residence rules should only be applied from the date of this realisation, not from the outset.[35]

29 Parker, H. (1997) *Money to Spend as they Wish: The Personal Expenses Allowance in Care Homes.* London: Age Concern England.

30 OFT (1998) Office of Fair Trading. *Older People as Consumers in Care Homes: A Report by the Office of Fair Trading.* London: OFT.

31 *Hampshire County Council 2001* (99/B/03979).

32 SI 1992/2977. *National Assistance (Assessment of Resources) Regulations 1992,* r.2.

33 *National Assistance Act 1948,* s.22. And: SI 1992/2977. *National Assistance (Assessment of Resources) Regulations 1992,* r.22(5A).

34 SI 1992/2977. National Assistance (Assessment of Resources) Regulations 1992.

35 Department of Health. (2009) *Charging for Residential Accommodation Guidance* ... paras 3.004–4A.

Local authorities might get this wrong or fail to explain it, and the local ombudsman might then find maladministration.[36]

If a care home placement is part of 'intermediate care', then it must anyway be free of charge to the resident for a period of up to six weeks (see Chapter 13).

LESS-DEPENDENT RESIDENTS

For people classed as 'less-dependent residents', authorities are explicitly given the option of not applying the normal charging rules at all. A less-dependent resident is defined as a person for whom accommodation is provided in premises not registered under the Care Standards Act 2000 (or, in future, the Health and Social Care Act 2008), that is where accomodation and personal care are not being provided together.[37] Factors the local authority should take account of include the resident's commitments (in relation to necessities such as food, fuel and clothing), independence, and incentive to become more independent.[38]

ASSESSMENT OF COUPLES

Local authorities are not empowered to apply the statutory means test under regulations to the spouse or partner of a resident. Each person entering residential care should be assessed individually, whether or not the other member of the couple is also a resident or remains at home. In other words, before being excluded from assistance on grounds of his or her capital resources, the resident must have (at the time of writing) in excess of £23,000 in *his or her own right*, whether separately or a share of jointly owned capital (see below).[39]

ASSESSING A PERSON'S CAPITAL ASSETS

Resources are assessed in terms of both capital and income. If a resident individually has more than a prescribed upper capital figure, then he or she will automatically pay the whole amount due and receive no financial support from the local authority. There is then no call to assess income. However, beneath that upper figure of (at time of writing) £23,000, but above a lower prescribed figure of £14,000, any capital over the lower figure is deemed to produce a weekly tariff income of

---

36 *Humberside County Council 1992* (91/C/0774).
37 SI 1992/2977. *National Assistance (Assessment of Resources) Regulations 1992*, rr.2, 5.
38 Department of Health (2009) *Charging for Residential Accommodation Guidance* … para 2.010.
39 Department of Health (2009) *Charging for Residential Accommodation Guidance* … paras 4.001–4.003.

£1 for every £250.[40] Over and above what this figure comes out at, the local authority will contribute the rest of the weekly fee charged for the accommodation.

Capital is not defined in legislation. Guidance states that capital, distinguished from income, is generally (a) not in respect of a specified period, and (b) not intended to form part of a series of payments. It lists, non-exhaustively, buildings, land, national savings certificates, premium bonds, stocks and shares, capital held by the Court of Protection[41] or a deputy it has appointed, building society accounts, bank accounts, SAYE schemes, unit trusts, trust funds, cash and Cooperative share accounts.[42]

WHOSE CAPITAL ASSET IS IT?

A capital asset normally belongs to the person in whose name it is held, that is, the *legal* owner. However, sometimes, somebody else will be the *beneficial* owner, in part or in whole. For instance, a resident may have £10,000 savings and £6500 in shares, but be able to show that the shares were bought on behalf of his son (who is abroad) and will be transferred to the son on his return. In which case, the son is the beneficial, though not yet legal, owner of the shares. The resident's capital therefore is confined to the £10,000 savings only.[43] For joint beneficial ownership of a capital asset, except for an interest in land, the total value should be divided equally between the owners.[44]

DISREGARDING CAPITAL IN THE MEANS TEST: RULES ABOUT PERSONAL INJURY COMPENSATION

Some capital is disregarded permanently, some temporarily. One of the rules applies to personal injury compensation. Local authorities frequently express frustration that they have to fund care, even when a person has a large compensation package. The rules are, however, not simple, and reference should be made to the Department of Health's *Charging for Residential Accommodation Guide* and the regulations.

Capital derived from a personal injury award and in a trust – or administered by, or under the direction of, a court – must be disregarded

---

40 SI 1992/2977. *National Assistance (Assessment of Resources) Regulations 1992*, rr.20, 28.
41 Under the Mental Capacity Act 2005 the Court of Protection makes decisions about the property, affairs, health care and welfare of people who lack capacity.
42 Department of Health (2009) *Charging for Residential Accommodation Guidance* ... para 6.002.
43 Department of Health (2009) *Charging for Residential Accommodation Guidance* ... para 6.008.
44 SI 1992/2977. *National Assistance (Assessment of Resources) Regulations 1992*, r.27.

indefinitely; likewise the value of the right to receive any income from such capital. Periodic payments for personal injury, made through a court order or agreement, 'to the extent that they are not a payment of income are treated as income (and disregarded in the calculation of income)'.[45]

Where the capital consists of any payment made in consequence of personal injury and a court has *not* specifically identified the payment covering the cost of providing care, that capital is disregarded for 52 weeks from the date of receipt of the first payment. However, if the money is placed in a disregarded location such as a personal injury trust or is administered by a court, disregards apply. Subsequent payments outside the 52 weeks are taken fully into account unless they are placed into a disregarded location.

Where the capital consists of any payment made in consequence of personal injury and a court *has* specifically identified the payment as being to cover the cost of providing care, that capital is taken into account. Nevertheless, if the money is placed in a disregarded location such as a personal injury trust or is administered by a court, disregards apply.[46]

AWARD OF PERSONAL INJURY DAMAGES
When damages are awarded against a defendant in personal injury negligence cases, they can be reduced if is clear that the local authority will in future meet the person's needs for care. However, the situation is complicated, because negligence law may demand that a person's needs be met to a higher standard than would be required under community care law.

Thus, the damages payable by a defendant may be reduced in recognition of what the local authority will in future provide – but then a 'top-up' be included, to reflect reasonable needs over and above local authority provision.[47] In 2009, the courts stated that in any case, a person should in principle be able to opt altogether for self-funding rather than rely on local authority provision. In which case, there would be no reduction in damages payable by the defendant, although the court would look to see that there was a safeguard against 'double

---

45 Department of Health (2009) *Charging for Residential Accommodation Guidance* ... paras 6.028.
46 Department of Health (2009) *Charging for Residential Accommodation Guidance* ... paras 10.025–10.025A.
47 *Sowden v Lodge* [2004] Civ EWCA 1370; *Godbold v Mahmood* [2005] EWHC 1002 QB; *Walton v Calderdale Healthcare NHS Trust* [2005] EWHC 1053 QB.

recovery' – that is, claiming the full damages and then still going to the local authority for assistance at a later date.[48]

DISREGARDING A PERSON'S HOME FOR 12 WEEKS

A person's dwelling must be disregarded for the first 12 weeks of a permanent resident's stay.[49] If the resident leaves residential care before the end of the 12 weeks and then re-enters on a permanent basis within 52 weeks, he or she is entitled to the balance of the 12-week disregard. If he or she re-enters more than 52 weeks later, the 12-week disregard applies afresh.[50]

(If the resident has acquired a home that he intends to move into, then it should be disregarded for up to 26 weeks or for a longer period if reasonable.)[51]

DISREGARDING THE PERSON'S HOME IF OTHER PEOPLE ARE LIVING IN IT

The value of the resident's home must be disregarded if it is occupied, whether wholly or partly:

(a) by the resident's partner or former partner (except in case of divorce or estrangement)

(b) by a lone parent who is the claimant's estranged or divorced partner

(c) by a relative or member of the family who is at least 60 years old, or who is under 16 years old and is liable to be maintained by the resident, or is incapacitated.

Apart from this mandatory disregard, if anybody else is living in the home, local authorities have discretion to disregard the property, if they 'consider it would be reasonable'.[52] Guidance suggests it might be reasonable in the case of a 'sole residence of someone who has given up their own home in order to care for the resident, or someone who is an elderly companion of the resident particularly if they have given up

---

48 *Peters v East Midlands Strategic Health Authority* [2009] EWCA Civ 145.

49 SI 1992/2977. *National Assistance (Assessment of Resources) Regulations 1992*, schedule 4, para 2. Also: schedule 3, para 10.

50 Department of Health (2009) *Charging for Residential Accommodation Guidance* ... para 7.003B.

51 SI 1992/2977. *National Assistance (Assessment of Resources) Regulations 1992*, schedule 4, para 18. And: Department of Health (2009) *Charging for Residential Accommodation Guidance* ... para 7.006.

52 SI 1992/2977. *National Assistance (Assessment of Resources) Regulations 1992*, schedule 4. And: Department of Health (2009) *Charging for Residential Accommodation Guidance* ... para 7.003.

their own home'. However, even then the authority could at a later date review the position – for example, when the carer has died or moved out.[53] It should be noted that the example given in the guidance is just that; the discretion is a wide one – although a local authority can clearly decide not to exercise it in appropriate circumstances.[54]

LEGAL AND BENEFICIAL OWNERS OF PROPERTY

There are circumstances in which the local authority might have difficulty taking account of the value of a property in which somebody else is living, if that person has a beneficial interest in it.

Guidance points out that legal owner means the person in whose name a property is held; beneficial owner means the person entitled to receive the proceeds or profits of the property. Normally the two will be one and the same, but not always. Where the care home resident is a legal owner of a property but has no beneficial interest in it, the property should not be taken into account for charging purposes. Conversely, if the resident has a beneficial interest in the property but is not the legal owner, then the property should be taken into account. Doubts about beneficial ownership might be resolved by considering the original intentions involved between the parties, in line with principles of the law of equity.[55]

The care home resident's share of the property should be valued at an amount equal to the price which his or her interest in possession would realise. However, this would be on the basis of it being sold to a willing buyer, and taking into account the likely effect on the price of somebody else with a beneficial interest (and in occupation). The price would also be less 10 per cent, representing the costs involved in selling.[56]

DEFERRING PAYMENT FOR CARE

Local authorities have a power to enter a 'deferred payment' arrangement with the resident.[57] This means that, when a local authority would be otherwise entitled to take account of a resident's home and force a sale,

53 Department of Health (2009) *Charging for Residential Accommodation Guidance* ... paras 7.007–8.
54 *R v Somerset County Council, ex p Harcombe* [1997] 96 LGR 444.
55 Department of Health (2009) *Charging for Residential Accommodation Guidance* ... paras 7.009–11, 7.014A.
56 SI 1992/2977. *National Assistance (Assessment of Resources) Regulations 1992*, r.27.
57 *Health and Social Care Act 2001*, s.54. And: SI 2001/3069. *National Assistance (Residential Accommodation) (Relevant Contributions) (England) Regulations 2001*.

it will not do so.[58] Instead, it can place a progressively increasing land charge for an agreed period (i.e. until the person dies or until the elapse of some other agreed period of time). This is so that people do not have to sell their homes during the period of the agreement.

Guidance stresses a number of points as follows.[59] Local authorities have discretion, not a duty, to enter a deferred payment agreement in any individual case. Authorities should ensure that the resident will have sufficient assets eventually to repay the money owing and meet other commitments (e.g. mortgage payments). If an authority enters into a high value agreement with one person, it might affect its ability to enter agreements with others. A deferred payment agreement only takes effect after the 12-week mandatory property disregard (see above).

Such agreements should not supplant the use of the discretion not to take account of the property at all, where there is somebody (such as a former carer) still living in it. An agreement lasts until the end of the exempt period, that is, 56 days after the resident dies, the end of an agreed period, or when it is otherwise terminated by the resident. The authority cannot terminate the agreement of its own accord. The debt is only payable, and interest only chargeable, from the day after the exempt period ends. The guidance also states that authorities should distinguish placing a charge on the property under a deferred payment agreement[60] from placing such a charge when the resident is simply failing to pay an assessed charge.[61]

Allowing a deferred payment agreement in any one case is a discretion only. But, clearly, the council needs to have a deferred payment policy and scheme in the first place, so that the possibility of an agreement with a particular resident is possible. The ombudsman has found maladministration when a council failed to have a scheme.[62] Department of Health guidance states that such a failure is unlawful;[63] yet one in five councils apparently doesn't operate such a scheme.[64]

58 SI 2001/3067. *National Assistance (Residential Accommodation) (Disregarding of Resources) (England) Regulations 2001.*

59 LAC(2001)25. Department of Health. *Charges for Residential Accommodation: CRAG Amendment No. 15.* London: DH, Annex.

60 *Health and Social Care Act 2001*, s.54.

61 *Health and Social Services and Social Security Adjudications Act 1983*, s.22.

62 *Manchester City Council 2005* (04/C/04804).

63 LAC(2009)3. Department of Health. *Charges for Residential Accommodation: CRAG Amendment No. 28.* London DH: para 15.

64 Hannam, L. (2009) 'Elderly forced to sell their homes to pay care costs.' Available at www.channel4.com/news/articles/society/elderly+forced+to+sell+homes+to+pay+care+costs/2913557, accessed on 4 September 2009.

NOTIONAL CAPITAL

In certain circumstances, a resident may be assessed as possessing capital – even though not actually in possession of it. This is called notional capital and might be capital (a) of which the resident has deprived himself or herself in order to decrease the amount payable for the accommodation, (b) which would be payable if he or she applied for it, or (c) which is paid to a third party in respect of the resident.

The rule that capital that would be available on application by the resident should be treated as belonging to him or her does not apply where that capital is held in a discretionary trust; a trust derived from a personal-injury compensation payment (or a court-administered sum arising from personal injury compensation), or a loan that could be raised against a capital asset (e.g. the person's home), which is being disregarded.[65]

GIVING ASSETS AWAY TO AVOID PAYING CARE HOME CHARGES

A local authority can treat a resident as still possessing a capital asset, and thus possessing notional capital, if it believes that the resident has deprived himself or herself of it, in order to reduce accommodation fees.[66] This is tantamount to pretending that a person has money that he or she does not possess, but is meant to be a disincentive for avoidance of care home fees.

Guidance states that avoiding the charge 'need not be the resident's main motive but it must be a significant one'. So it would not be reasonable for the authority to argue deprivation if the resident was, at the time of the disposal, 'fit and healthy and could not have foreseen the need for a move to residential accommodation'.[67] There is no rule about how long ago the deprivation must have occurred. However, the greater the period between the deprivation and the entry into the care home, the more difficult for the local authority to argue relevant motive.

If deprivation of capital is shown, the local authority can attempt to recover the assessed charge owing from the resident as normal. Alternatively, if the resident cannot pay, then in some circumstances the third party to whom the asset was transferred will be liable – but only

---

65 Department of Health (2009) *Charging for Residential Accommodation Guidance* ... paras 6.049–6.053.
66 SI 1992/2977. *National Assistance (Assessment of Resources) Regulations 1992*, r.25. And: Department of Health (2009). *Charging for residential accommodation guidance* ... paras 6.052–3, 6.057.
67 Department of Health (2009) *Charging for residential accommodation guidance* ... para 6.064.

if the deprivation took place less than six months before the person was placed by the local authority in the care home.[68]

PRACTICALITIES OF DEMANDING NOTIONAL CAPITAL
Demanding payment, notwithstanding deprivation, will be fruitless if the resident does not have actual, as opposed to notional, capital – and if the third party is not liable because the asset was transferred over six months before the resident entered the care home.[69] (But see below for insolvency proceedings.)

An incentive for identifying notional capital would be for the local authority to argue that it has no duty to contract for the care home placement at all – on the grounds that the person has the money (theoretically) to make his or her own arrangements. Then, the resident could in principle be evicted for non-payment. The Scottish courts were prepared to countenance this happening in the case of a woman with dementia. However, the House of Lords overturned the decision and ruled that in Scotland at least this would not be lawful; and that local authorities would be obliged to continue to fund the care home placement.[70] The position in England is likely to be the same.

ASSESSMENT OF INCOME
A payment of income (other than earnings: see below) is generally distinguished from capital on the basis that it is made in relation to a period and is part of a series (regular or irregular) of payments.[71] As with capital, income might be wholly or partly disregarded, or be taken fully into account. Residents may also be assessed as having notional income if, for example, they have deprived themselves of income in order to reduce the charge payable.

TAKING ACCOUNT OF INCOME
One of the rules about income applies when a local authority places a person in a higher cost home, on the basis of a third party topping up the excess. Any lump sum payment made by the third party should be

---

68 SI 1992/2977. *National Assistance (Assessment of Resources) Regulations 1992*, r.25. And: Department of Health (2009) *Charging for Residential Accommodation Guidance* … para 6.067.
69 *Health and Social Services and Social Security Adjudications Act 1983*, s.21.
70 *Robertson v Fife Council* [2002] UKHL 35, House of Lords.
71 Department of Health (2009) *Charging for Residential Accommodation Guidance* … paras 8.001–2.

divided by the number of weeks for which the payment is made – and then taken into account fully as the resident's income.

During the 12-week property disregard or during a deferred payments agreement, the resident may himself or herself be paying towards a higher price home. The payment made by the resident should be treated as part of his or her income. If made as a lump sum, it should be divided by the number of weeks for which the payment is made and then taken into account fully as the resident's income.[72]

DISREGARDING INCOME: PERSONAL INJURY COMPENSATION

The rules about this are not simple, and reference should be made to the Department of Health's *Charging for Residential Accommodation Guide* and the regulations. Broadly, income from capital is generally (but not always) treated as capital and not income. So, if there is any disregard under the rules for capital (see above), then it will apply to any such income. In particular, however, periodic payments at regular intervals in relation to personal injury are disregarded in the case of personal injury trust funds, payments under an annuity through any agreement or court order, or payments through any agreement or court order.[73]

PURSUIT OF DEBT

Local authorities are empowered under the National Assistance Act 1948, without prejudice to any other method of recovery, to recover money owing for care home fees, as a civil debt – within three years of the sum becoming due.[74]

PURSUING PAYMENT FROM A THIRD PARTY

Local authorities are empowered to pursue money owing to them from a third party – to whom the resident transferred assets not more than six months before entry into residential accommodation. This must have been done knowingly and with the intention of avoiding charges for the accommodation. The transfer needs to have been at an under value or for no consideration at all.[75]

This six-month rule is only triggered when the local authority has assessed the person as needing residential accommodation under Part III

72 SI 1992/2977. *National Assistance (Assessment of Resources) Regulations 1992*, r.16A.
73 Department of Health (2009) *Charging for Residential Accommodation Guidance* ... paras 8.015, 10.026.
74 *National Assistance Act 1948*, s.56.
75 *Health and Social Services and Social Security Adjudications Act 1983*, s.21.

of the 1948 Act, and has arranged a placement. The rule does not apply if the resident is self-funding in an independent sector home, has not been assessed, or has not had his or her placement arranged by the local authority.[76]

PLACING A LEGAL LAND CHARGE ON THE PROPERTY FOR MONEY OWING

If a resident fails to pay charges for accommodation, the local authority is empowered to place a charge on any land or property in which the resident has a beneficial interest. The charge will only bear interest from the day after the resident dies. The rate of interest should be a reasonable one as directed by the Secretary of State; otherwise, as the local authority determines.[77]

INSOLVENCY PROCEEDINGS

If local authorities attempt to enforce charges, but the person being pursued has no or little money left (e.g. following a deliberate deprivation of resources), they clearly have a problem. Authorities might then consider proceedings under the Insolvency Act 1986 to enable them to pursue a third party (to whom the asset was transferred).

First, steps might be taken to have the resident declared bankrupt, in which case any of the resident's transactions made at an under value in the past two years can be set aside[78] (or in the past five years – in the unlikely event that the resident was already insolvent at the time of the transaction).

Second, a gift, no matter how long ago it was made, can be set aside if the court is convinced that the purpose (not necessarily sole or even dominant, but at least substantial) of the gift was to place the assets beyond the reach of a possible creditor or otherwise prejudice a creditor's interests[79] (e.g. to avoid paying residential care charges). However, this test does not necessarily mean that a transaction designed primarily to minimise tax liabilities would fall foul of this legal rule s.423.[80]

---

76 Department of Health (2009) *Charging for Residential Accommodation Guidance* ... Annex D.
77 *Health and Social Services and Social Security Adjudications Act 1983*, ss.22, 24.
78 *Insolvency Act 1986*, ss.339–441.
79 *Insolvency Act 1986*, ss.423–425.
80 *Law Society v Southall* [2001] EWCA Civ 2001. But contrast: *Derbyshire County Council v Akrill* [2005] EWCA Civ 308.

CHAPTER 6

Community care services: help in people's own homes

- Advice, support, social rehabilitation, etc: National Assistance Act 1948, s.29
  - Definition of disability
  - Substantial and permanent handicap
- Services for disabled people: Chronically Sick and Disabled Persons Act 1970, s.2
  - Practical assistance in the home, travel, equipment, home adaptations, holidays, etc.
  - Strong duty under the CSDPA 1970
  - Practical assistance in and around the home
  - Recreational facilities
  - Taking advantage of educational facilities
  - Home adaptations and additional facilities for greater safety, comfort or convenience
  - Holidays
- Information provision about services
- Services for older people: Health Services and Public Health Act 1968, s.45
- Illness, mental disorder, home help, etc: NHS Act 2006
  - Services for illness
  - Home help and laundry facilities
  - Expectant and nursing mothers
- Aftercare services: Mental Health Act 1983, s.117
  - Who is entitled to aftercare services?
  - Responsible bodies for providing aftercare services
  - Range of aftercare services

- Strength of duty to provide aftercare services
- Ending aftercare services
- Charging for aftercare services
- Charging for non-residential services generally
  - Services that can be charged for
  - Services that cannot be charged for
  - Reasonableness of charge
  - Reasonable practicability of person paying the charge
  - Appeal and review procedure: adequate information
  - Department of Health guidance on charging
    - No presumption of charging
    - Avoid impoverishing people
    - Taking account of people's disability benefits as income
    - Assessing people's disability-related expenditure before deciding what they can afford to pay
  - Day and night services
  - Taking account of people's capital assets
  - Personal-injury compensation payments
  - Whose resources can be taken into account?
  - Disregarding earnings
  - Full cost of the service
  - Carers
  - Direct payments
  - NHS payments
  - Refusal to pay charge
  - Refusal to disclose resources
  - Consultation about charges
  - Scope of review in considering reasonable practicability of person paying the assessed charge

SUMMARY

The provision of non-residential community care services is governed by assessment conducted under s.47 of the NHS and Community Care Act 1990. These services are not contained within the 1990 Act itself, but, instead, are scattered across five other pieces of legislation.

The services are wide ranging and of enormous potential assistance to people. They include social work services, advice, support, holidays, practical assistance in the home, assistance to take advantage of educational facilities, recreational activities, additional facilities (equipment), home adaptations, holidays, night-sitter services, home help, laundry service, visiting services, assistance in finding accommodation, etc.

Less helpfully, the extent, overlap and fragmentation of the legislation tend to feed the uncertainty outlined in Chapter 2. Not only are service users often unaware of what services could or must be provided, but so, too, are local authority staff. Local authorities have in any case rationed these services drastically, under the government policy of 'fair access to care', by imposing ever stricter thresholds of eligibility for services (see Chapter 4).

ADVICE, SUPPORT, SOCIAL REHABILITATION, ETC: NATIONAL ASSISTANCE ACT 1948, S.29

A number of non-residential services for disabled people are listed under s.29 of the National Assistance Act 1948. By means of directions and approvals passed by the Secretary of State, a duty applies for people ordinarily resident within a local authority; otherwise there is only a power to provide these services.[1] The services are:

(a) compiling and maintaining a *register of disabled people*

(b) providing a social work service and such advice and support as is needed for people at home or elsewhere

(c) providing, whether at centres or elsewhere, facilities for *social rehabilitation and adjustment to disability*, including assistance in overcoming limitations of mobility or communication

(d) providing, either at centres or elsewhere, facilities for *occupational, social, cultural and recreational activities* – and, where appropriate, payments to persons for work they have done.

The duty is regarded by the courts as a specific, strong duty and therefore is enforceable.[2] The local ombudsman has found maladministration for failure to provide adequate social work support,[3] adequate advice and assistance[4] or social rehabilitation.[5]

1   LAC(93)10. Department of Health. *Approvals and Directions for Arrangements from 1st April 2003 Made Under Schedule 8 to the NHS Act 1977 and Sections 21 and 29 of the National Assistance Act 1948.* London: DH, Appendix 2.
2   *R (Manchester City Council) v St. Helens Borough Council* [2009] EWCA Civ 1348.
3   *Buckinghamshire County Council 1992* (90/B/1340).
4   *Stockton-on-Tees Borough Council 1997 and the former Stockton-on-Tees Borough Council and the former Cleveland County Council* (96/C/1523 and others).
5   *Manchester City Council 1993* (90/C/2147).

DEFINITION OF DISABILITY

A basic condition of eligibility for the provision of non-residential services under s.29 of the 1948 Act (and under the Chronically Sick and Disabled Persons Act 1970, s.2) is that the person be disabled. The language used is, however, generally regarded as anachronistic. It refers to a person being (a) blind, deaf or dumb, (b) having a permanent and substantial handicap through illness, injury or congenital deformity, or (c) having a mental disorder of any description.

SUBSTANTIAL AND PERMANENT HANDICAP

First, Department of Health statutory guidance points out that it is disability, not registration of that disability, which is a condition for provision of service. Second, for people with blindness or partial sight, the guidance refers to the established procedure of medical certification and local authority registration.[6] For people with hearing impairment, it states that the 'deaf' category should include people who are deaf with speech, deaf without speech, or hard of hearing (that is, those who, with or without a hearing aid, have some useful hearing and whose normal method of communication is by speech, listening and lip-reading).

Third, the guidance states that it is not possible to give precise guidance on the interpretation of the phrase 'substantially and permanently handicapped'. However, it asks local authorities to give a wide interpretation to the term 'substantial', which should always 'take full account of individual circumstances'. With regard to the term 'permanent', it states that authorities would wish to interpret this 'sufficiently flexibly to ensure that they do not feel inhibited from giving help under s.29 in cases where they are uncertain of the likely duration of the condition'.[7]

SERVICES FOR DISABLED PEOPLE: CHRONICALLY SICK AND DISABLED PERSONS ACT 1970, S.2

Under s.2 of the Chronically Sick and Disabled Persons Act 1970 (CSDPA), a local authority has a duty, if certain conditions are met, to arrange non-residential services for disabled people. The 1970 Act extends s.29 of the National Assistance Act 1948.[8]

---

6   Department of Health (2003) *Identification, Referral and Registration of Sight Loss: Action for Social Services Department and Optometrists, and Explanatory Notes.* London: DH.

7   LAC(93)10. Department of Health. *Approvals and Directions* ... Appendix 4.

8   *R v Powys County Council, ex p Hambidge* [1998] 1 CCLR 458, Court of Appeal.

The conditions are that (a) the local authority has functions under s.29 of the 1948 Act (i.e. the person be disabled), (b) the person is ordinarily resident in the authority's area, (c) the person has a need, and (d) the local authority is satisfied that it is necessary, in order to meet that need, for it to arrange services. In addition, the local authority must act under the general guidance of the Secretary of State issued under s.7(1) of the Local Authority Social Services Act 1970.

PRACTICAL ASSISTANCE IN THE HOME, TRAVEL, EQUIPMENT, HOME ADAPTATIONS, HOLIDAYS, ETC.

The services listed in the CSDPA 1970 are extensive (italics added):

(a) provision of *practical assistance* for the person in his or her home

(b) provision of or assistance to the person in obtaining *wireless, television, library* or similar recreational facilities

(c) provision for the person of *lectures, games, outings or other recreational facilities* outside his or her home or assistance to that person in taking advantage of *educational facilities* available to him or her

(d) provision for the person of facilities for, or assistance in, *travelling* to and from his or her home for the purpose of participating in any services provided under s.29 (National Assistance Act 1948) or in any other similar services

(e) provision of assistance for the person in arranging for the carrying out of any *works of adaptation* in his or her home or the provision of any *additional facilities* designed to secure his or her greater safety, comfort or convenience

(f) facilitating the taking of *holidays* by the person, whether at holiday homes or otherwise and whether provided under arrangements made by the authority or otherwise

(g) provision of *meals* for that person whether in his or her home or elsewhere

(h) provision for that person of, or assistance to that person in obtaining, a *telephone* and any special equipment necessary to enable him or her to use a telephone.

STRONG DUTY UNDER THE CSDPA 1970

The duty to arrange services is strong and legally enforceable by individuals. The courts have held that, once a person is deemed to have an eligible need, then a lack of resources will not excuse a failure to meet that need.[9] The reason for this strength of duty lies in the fact that s.2 of the 1970 Act refers to 'any person' and states that, once the local authority is satisfied that it is necessary to meet the need of that person, it must do so by providing any or all of the services listed.

PRACTICAL ASSISTANCE IN AND AROUND THE HOME

Practical assistance in the home is a broad term that could range from a small amount of home help each week, to full-scale personal assistance 24 hours a day. Local authorities should be wary of generally excluding low-level services; to do so is contrary to statutory guidance and risks maladministration or unlawfulness (see Chapter 4).

RECREATIONAL FACILITIES

When one local authority ruled out, as a matter of policy, providing for a person's social, recreational and leisure needs – stating that the person could arrange these for him- or herself – this was unlawful.[10]

TAKING ADVANTAGE OF EDUCATIONAL FACILITIES

The duty concerning educational facilities is not about actually making arrangements for the provision of education, but about assisting the person to take advantage of what is already potentially available.[11] Department of Health guidance states that such assistance could cover, for instance, personal care that might be required to assist a person study – in addition to any educational disabled-student allowance awarded.[12]

HOME ADAPTATIONS AND ADDITIONAL FACILITIES FOR GREATER SAFETY, COMFORT OR CONVENIENCE

Home adaptations are covered in Chapter 12 of this book. The term 'additional facilities' is broad and covers, among other things, the wide range of daily living equipment that local authorities provide. The

9   *R v Gloucestershire County Council, ex p Barry* [1997] 2 All ER 1, House of Lords.

10 *R v Haringey London Borough Council, ex p Norton* [1998] 1 CCLR 168.

11 *R v Further Education Funding Council and Bradford Metropolitan District Council, ex p Parkinson* [1997] 2 FCR 67.

12 LAC(93)12. Department of Health. *Further and Higher Education Act 1992: Implications for Sections 5 and 6 of the Disabled Persons (Services, Consultation and Representation) Act 1986.* London: DH, paras 9–10.

purpose of such facilities is also broad: not just safety, but also comfort and convenience. In one case, the local ombudsman referred not only to the potential danger, but also to the 'extreme discomfort' and the 'inconvenient' accommodation, in which a disabled woman had to live – while waiting four years and eight months for the simple aids that eventually made such a difference to her life.[13]

HOLIDAYS
Local authorities, thinking perhaps that these were trivial as opposed to essential breaks for people, have lost several legal cases because of over-restrictive policies on holidays.[14]

INFORMATION PROVISION ABOUT SERVICES
Local authorities have a specific duty under s.1 of the CSDPA 1970 to inform existing service users about other services that the authority thinks relevant and which it knows about. This is a strong duty that a local authority has towards individual people. The local ombudsman has found maladministration in relation to the giving of poor advice about social security benefits[15] or about home adaptations.[16]

SERVICES FOR OLDER PEOPLE: HEALTH SERVICES AND PUBLIC HEALTH ACT 1968, S.45
By means of approvals made by the Secretary of State under s.45 of the Health Services and Public Health Act 1968, local authorities have a *power* but not a duty to make arrangements for promoting the welfare of old people. The power is so wide and older people so numerous that no government has ever changed the power into a duty – although the legislation does allow for the passing of directions that would bring this about. The arrangements are (italics added):

(a) provision of *meals and recreation* in the home and elsewhere

(b) *informing* the elderly of services available to them and to identify elderly people in need of services

---

13 *Hackney London Borough Council 1992* (91/A/0482).

14 *R v Ealing London Borough Council, ex p Leaman* [1984] TLR, 10 February 1984; *R v North Yorkshire County Council, ex p Hargreaves (no.2)* [1997] 96 LGR 39; *R(B) v Cornwall County Council* [2009] EWHC 491 (Admin).

15 *East Sussex County Council 1995* (93/A/3738).

16 *Leicester City Council 1992 and Leicestershire County Council* (91/B/0254 and 91/B/0380).

(c) providing facilities or assistance in *travelling* to and from the home for the purpose of participating in services provided by the authority or similar services

(d) assisting in finding suitable *households for boarding* elderly persons

(e) providing *visiting and advisory services and social work support*

(f) providing *practical assistance in the home* including assistance in the carrying out of *works of adaptation* or the provision of any *additional facilities* designed to secure greater safety, comfort or convenience

(g) contributing to the cost of employing a *warden* on welfare functions in warden-assisted housing schemes and to provide warden services for occupiers of private housing.

This list represents a wide range of services and assistance that local authorities may, but are not obliged to, provide for older people. Department of Health guidance states that the purpose of s.45 is to enable authorities to help elderly people who are not significantly disabled. This is to promote the welfare of the elderly generally and, so far as possible, prevent or postpone personal or social deterioration or breakdown.[17]

ILLNESS, MENTAL DISORDER, HOME HELP, ETC: NHS ACT 2006

By means of directions and approvals made by the Secretary of State, local authorities have powers and duties to arrange services under s.254 and schedule 20 of the NHS Act 2006.[18] The services relate to illness, home help for households and to expectant and nursing mothers.

SERVICES FOR ILLNESS

Non-residential services are covered for the prevention of illness, the care of people who are ill, and the aftercare of people who have been ill. Illness is defined as including 'mental disorder within the meaning of the Mental Health Act 1983 and any injury or disability requiring

---

17 DHSS 19/71. Department of Health and Social Security. *Welfare of the Elderly: Implementation of Section 45 of the Health Services and Public Health Act 1945.* London: DHSS.

18 LAC(93)10. Department of Health. *Approvals and Directions* ... Appendix 3.

medical or dental treatment or nursing'.[19] There is a duty towards people with a mental disorder (italics added):

(a) provision of *centres* (including training centres and day centres) for the training or occupation of such people

(b) the exercise of local authority functions towards people received into *guardianship* under Part 2 or 3 of the Mental Health Act 1983

(c) provision of *social work and related services* to help in the identification, diagnosis, assessment and social treatment of mental disorder and to provide social work support and other domiciliary and care services to people living in their homes or elsewhere.

These services appear to be covered only by a general, target duty, rather than a specific one. It is therefore likely that legally enforcing provision would be difficult. In addition are powers to arrange services in respect of illness generally. The services comprise arrangements for the provision of (italics added):

(a) *centres* or other facilities for training or keeping people suitably occupied, to equip and maintain such centres, and for the provision of ancillary or supplemental services

(b) *meals* at centres and at other facilities, and meals on wheels for housebound people

(c) *remuneration* of people engaged in suitable work at centres or at other facilities

(d) social services (including *advice and support*) in order to prevent the impairment of physical or mental health of adults in families where such impairment is likely, or to prevent the break-up of such families, or for assisting in their rehabilitation

(e) *night-sitter* services

(f) *recuperative holidays*, facilities for *social and recreational activities*

(g) services specifically for *alcoholic or drug-dependent people.*[20]

---

19 *NHS Act 2006*, s.275.
20 LAC(93)10. Department of Health. *Approvals and Directions* ... Appendix 3.

HOME HELP AND LAUNDRY FACILITIES

Local authorities also have a general duty to arrange, on a scale adequate for their area, home help – and a power to provide or arrange laundry facilities – for households where it is required because there is somebody who is ill, lying in, an expectant mother, or is aged or handicapped as a result of having suffered from illness or congenital deformity. The power to arrange the laundry facilities is dependent on the household either receiving, or being eligible to receive, the home help.[21]

Assistance is for the household, suggesting that it could be made for other members of the household, not just the disabled, aged or ill person. However, the duty is probably to be regarded as a general, target one and therefore difficult to enforce in individual cases.

EXPECTANT AND NURSING MOTHERS

Local authorities also have the power to make arrangements for the care of expectant and nursing mothers, other than for residential accommodation.[22]

AFTERCARE SERVICES: MENTAL HEALTH ACT 1983, S.117

NHS primary care trusts or health authorities, and local social services authorities – in cooperation with voluntary organisations – have a duty to provide aftercare services free of charge, when certain categories of patient detained in hospital under the Mental Health Act 1983 are discharged from hospital. This includes patients leaving hospital, even if they had previously ceased to be detained but remained in hospital as informal patients. The duty persists until the primary care trust or health authority and the local authority are satisfied that such services are no longer required.[23]

Local authorities have sometimes made considerable efforts to get around the rules about not charging people, and this has led to a major legal case to clarify the position. In addition, the local ombudsman has uncovered maladministration in a number of cases.

---

21 LAC(93)10. Department of Health. *Approvals and Directions* ... Appendix 3.
22 LAC(93)10. Department of Health. *Approvals and Directions* ... Appendix 3.
23 *Mental Health Act 1983*, s.117.

WHO IS ENTITLED TO AFTERCARE SERVICES?

The aftercare duty applies to people who have been detained under the 1983 Act, under s.3 (treatment), s.37 (convicted offenders with hospital or guardianship orders), or s.47 and s.48 (prisoners – serving a sentence, on remand, civil prisoners, people detained under the Immigration Act 1971 – for whom a transfer direction has been made).

Informal mental health patients are not covered. The duty does, however, apply to people granted leave of absence under s.17 of the 1983 Act – and to people transferred into guardianship (via s.19 of the 1983 Act), having originally been detained under s.3.[24]

RESPONSIBLE BODIES FOR PROVIDING AFTERCARE SERVICES

The responsible primary care trust, health authority and local authority are those for the area in which the person is resident – or for the area to which he or she is sent on discharge.[25] This means the responsible bodies are those where the person was resident at the time of detention. However, if there was no (ascertainable) place of residence at the time of detention, then the responsibility lies with those relevant bodies in the area to which the person is discharged.[26]

RANGE OF AFTERCARE SERVICES

Services under s.117 are effectively undefined and comprise both residential and non-residential provision. The Mental Health Act Code of Practice lists the following non-exhaustively: daytime activities or employment, appropriate accommodation, outpatient treatment, counselling and personal support, assistance with welfare rights and managing finances.[27] Section 117 implicitly contains these services; it is not merely a gateway to services provided under other legislation.[28]

STRENGTH OF DUTY TO PROVIDE AFTERCARE SERVICES

As explained in Chapter 3, there is a difference between individual, strong duties and general, weaker or target duties. Thus, s.117 places a strong duty on the NHS, in contrast to the less specific duty to provide

---

24 *R v Manchester City Council, ex p Stennett* (1999) 2 CCLR 402.

25 *Mental Health Act 1983*, s.117.

26 *R v Mental Health Review Tribunal, Torfaen County Borough Council and Gwent Health Authority, ex p Hall* (1999) 2 CCLR 361. See also: local ombudsman investigation: *Wigan Metropolitan Borough Council and Medway Council 2008* (06/B/12247, 06/B/12248).

27 Department of Health (2008) *Code of Practice: Mental Health Act 1983*. London: Department of Health, para 27.12.

28 *R v Manchester City Council, ex p Stennett* [2002] UKHL 34, House of Lords.

aftercare under s.3 of the NHS Act 2006.[29] The duty placed by s.117 on local social services authorities is likewise a stronger duty than the general duty to provide aftercare for mentally disordered people under schedule 254 of the NHS Act 2006.

The courts have stated that the s.117 duty is to exercise reasonable endeavours. The duty must be performed (assuming no genuinely insuperable obstacle), but the nature and extent of the aftercare services falls, to a degree, within the discretion of the primary care trust, which must have regard to other demands on its budget.[30]

ENDING AFTERCARE SERVICES

The legal requirement not to charge for s.117 services (see below) means there is an incentive for a local authority to discharge the person from his or her s.117 status, but to continue to provide services through other legislation under which financial charges *can* be made. But caution is required.

First, the decision to discharge s.117 is a joint one. It arguably cannot be made unilaterally. Therefore the ombudsman found maladministration when a local authority based its decision solely on what the NHS stated; the authority had not formed its own judgement as a social services authority.[31]

Second, local authorities sometimes take the view that s.117 can be discharged if the service user has become stable in the community and is unlikely to require readmission to hospital. Taken as a decisive indicator, this is suspect, because the fact that the aftercare services are meeting the need does not mean they are no longer required. If anything, it may be the opposite; and the courts have stated that the persistence of the mental disorder may well mean that aftercare services must continue.[32]

The local ombudsman considered this issue in the case of a woman whose care home placement was recategorised away from free s.117 aftercare to the National Assistance Act 1948 (under which she would have to pay). This was on the basis of her stability in the care home. The ombudsman rejected this approach. The correct question was whether removal of the person (settled or not) from the care home would risk

---

29   *R v Ealing District Health Authority, ex p Fox* [1993] WLR 373.
30   *R(K) v Camden and Islington Health Authority* [2001] EWCA Civ 240.
31   *Clwyd County Council 1997* (97/0177, 97/0755).
32   *R v Manchester City Council, ex p Stennett* (1999) 2 CCLR 402.

readmission to hospital. If the answer was 'yes' then the person could not be discharged from aftercare.[33]

More generally, the local ombudsmen have criticised local authorities for attempting to discharge s.117 without performing a proper review and consulting the person and his or her carer in accordance with Department of Health guidance.[34] Some of the ombudsman investigations suggest at best a lack of interest in applying the law, and at worst underhand practices by local authorities in respect of vulnerable people.[35]

CHARGING FOR AFTERCARE SERVICES

The courts held in 1999 that charges under s.117 are not lawful.[36] This caught out the many local authorities that had been charging for such services over a long period of time. As a consequence, they now owed substantial sums of money to relevant service users whom they had unlawfully charged. For instance, in one local government ombudsman investigation, the ombudsman recommended that the local authority reimburse £60,000 to one person.[37] In another instance, the ombudsmen reported the sum owing to a person as £294,000.[38]

The local ombudsmen became aware that local authorities were in some cases attempting to avoid paying money back, either by retrospectively discharging people from s.117, or employing restrictive cut-off dates for money owing. As a consequence, the ombudsmen issued their own guidance on how local authorities should go about paying money back.[39]

Notwithstanding this controversy, local authorities continue to try to find a way around the rules. In one case an authority attempted to place a woman in a cheaper care home that would meet neither her assessed needs nor the requirements of a care plan. If she wished to go into the more expensive home, she would have to top up. The ombudsman found maladministration; the local authority should have

---

33 *Bath and North East Somerset Council 2007* (06/B/16774).

34 HSC 2000/3; LAC(2000)3. Department of Health. *After-care Under the Mental Health Act 1983.* London: DH.

35 *Wiltshire County Council 1999* (98/B/0341); *Leicestershire County Council 2001* (00/B/08307); *Poole Borough Council 2007* (06/B/07542); *Hounslow London Borough Council 1995* (93/A/3007).

36 *R v Manchester City Council, ex p Stennett* [2002] UKHL 34, House of Lords.

37 *Wiltshire County Council 1999* (98/B/0341).

38 Commission for Local Administration in England (2004) *Local Government Ombudsman: Annual Report 2003/4.* London: CLAE, p.7.

39 Commission for Local Administration (2003) *Special Report: Advice and Guidance on the Funding of Aftercare Under Section 117 of the Mental Health Act 1983.* London: CLAE.

covered the cost of a care home that would meet her needs.[40] In a second, seemingly extraordinary, case, the local authority persuaded the patient to sign away her statutory right to free placement under s.117 in a care home. Having done so, she was then effectively forced to pay full cost for the placement.[41]

CHARGING FOR NON-RESIDENTIAL SERVICES GENERALLY

Local authorities have only a power rather than a duty to charge for non-residential services.[42] This is under s.17 of the Health and Social Services and Social Security Adjudications Act 1983 (HASSASSA). Unusually for a power, it is used extensively and diversely. For instance, the maximum weekly charge a local authority might make varies between authorities from £23.50 to £400.00.[43] A third of local authorities do not have a maximum charge, and, at a rate of up to £17.30 an hour, care charges can be high.[44]

Furthermore, as boundaries between health and social care blur, the redefining of certain services as 'social' rather than 'health' care can result in services such as bathing or respite care, previously provided free of charge by the NHS, now being charged for by local authorities. It remains important that – despite central government's insistence on joint working and 'seamless' services – there should be clarity as to which part of a care package is health care and which social care. This will avoid unlawful charging for those health care services that should be free. For instance, a current bone of contention in many areas is whether medication-associated visits should be classed as health or social care.

Overall, local authorities display increasing financial rapaciousness, with detrimental consequences to vulnerable older people being reported. For example, in order to afford the charges people cut back on other matters affecting their well-being, including going out less, not being able to afford transport costs, stopping education classes, stopping or reducing activities such as swimming and physiotherapy, and cutting back on food and heating.[45]

---

40 *North Yorkshire County Council 2007* (05/C/13158).
41 *York City Council 2006* (04/B/01280).
42 *Health and Social Services and Social Security Adjudications Act 1983*, s.17.
43 Coalition on Charging (2008) *Charging into Poverty?* London: Coalition on Charging, p.11.
44 Counsel and Care (2007) *Care Contradictions: Higher Charges and Fewer Services.* London: Counsel and Care, p.8.
45 Coalition on Charging (2008) *Charging into Poverty?* London: Coalition on Charging, p.22.

SERVICES THAT CAN BE CHARGED FOR

Non-residential services that can be charged for under s.17 of the 1983 Act are: National Assistance Act 1948 (s.29: welfare arrangements for disabled people), Health Services and Public Health Act 1968 (s.45: welfare of old people), NHS Act 2006 (schedule 20: prevention of illness, care and aftercare, home help and laundry facilities), Carers and Disabled Children Act 2000 (services for carers). By extension, s.2 of the Chronically Sick and Disabled Persons Act 1970 is also covered.

SERVICES THAT CANNOT BE CHARGED FOR

Some non-residential services cannot be charged for. Thus central government guidance states that community care assessment should not be charged for. In any case, s.47 of the NHS and Community Care Act 1990 is not listed as a chargeable service under s.17 of the HASSASSA 1983. The guidance also states that advice about services should not be charged for.[46] And the courts have made clear that aftercare services under s.117 of the Mental Health Act 1983 cannot be charged for.[47]

In addition, other legislation prohibits charges being made for provision of any community equipment (whatever it costs to provide), or for any minor adaptations costing £1000 or less.[48] Guidance states that the cost of such minor adaptations can be calculated to include buying and fitting, and that councils retain the discretion to charge for minor adaptations that exceed £1000 in cost.[49] The same legislation also states that, for up to six weeks, intermediate care cannot be charged for (see Chapter 13). The Personal Care Bill 2009, if it becomes law, will make provision for free care to be provided for an indefinite period for at least some people living in their own homes.

REASONABLENESS OF CHARGE

Any charge imposed must be reasonable.[50] The courts have held that this is a broad, flexible test.[51] Nonetheless, the local ombudsman has found maladministration in relation to arbitrary rules on charging and also

---

46 Department of Health (2003) *Fairer charging policies for home and other non-residential social services: guidance for councils with social services responsibilities.* London: DH, para 8.
47 *R v Manchester City Council, ex p Stennett* [2002] UKHL 34, House of Lords.
48 SI 2003/1196. *Community Care (Delayed Discharges) (Qualifying Services) (England) Regulations 2003.*
49 LAC(2003)14. Department of Health. *Changes to Local Authorities' Charging Regime for Community Equipment and Intermediate Care Services.* London: DH.
50 *Health and Social Services and Social Security Adjudications Act 1983*, s.17.
51 *Avon County Council v Hooper* [1997] 1 All ER 532, Court of Appeal.

when staff have not known what their own local authority's rules on charging actually were.[52]

REASONABLE PRACTICABILITY OF PERSON PAYING THE CHARGE

If a person satisfies the local authority that it is not reasonably practicable for him or her to pay the assessed charge, the authority should reduce the charge to a level at which it is reasonably practicable for the person to pay.[53]

The courts have stated that it is for the service user to 'discharge his burden of persuasion' by showing that he or she has insufficient means to pay; and that 'means' applies not just to cash but also to other realisable assets.[54] However, the local ombudsman considers that the word 'hardship' is not a simple substitute for 'reasonable practicability', suggesting that the latter is of wider scope. Furthermore, the ombudsman will look for reasoned, rather than arbitrary, decision-making when reasonable practicability is considered. For instance, it is not good enough if a service user's breakdown of expenditure is doubted, without the local authority being familiar with the needs of the person.[55]

The courts have also have pulled local authorities up for rigid or irrational approaches to what it is reasonably practicable for a person to pay.[56]

APPEAL AND REVIEW PROCEDURE: ADEQUATE INFORMATION

One way in which the service user can discharge the burden of convincing the authority about the unaffordability of a charge is to take advantage of appeal procedures. The local ombudsman has emphasised that a local authority should provide adequate information and procedures so as to give the person a decent chance of doing this.[57]

---

52 *Essex County Council 1991* (90/A/2675); *Durham County Council 2000* (99/C/1983).

53 *Health and Social Services and Social Security Adjudications Act 1983, s.17.*

54 *Avon County Council v Hooper* [1997] 1 All ER 532, Court of Appeal.

55 *Gateshead Metropolitan Borough Council 2001* (99/C/02509, 99/C/02624).

56 *R(Stephenson) v Stockton-on-Tees Borough Council* [2005] EWCA Civ 960; *R(B) v Cornwall County Council* [2009] EWHC 491 (Admin); *R(Carton) v Coventry City Council* (2001) 4 CCLR 41.

57 *Derbyshire County Council 2004* (02/C/14235 and others); *Gateshead Metropolitan Borough Council 2001* (99/C/02509, 99/C/02624); *Greenwich London Borough Council 1993* (91/A/3782); *Essex County Council 1991* (90/A/2675).

DEPARTMENT OF HEALTH GUIDANCE ON CHARGING

The Audit Commission reported in 2000 on home care charges. It found significant inconsistencies across the country and also disadvantages suffered by people on the lowest incomes but with the highest costs related to their disability.[58] In response, the Department of Health issued detailed, statutory (i.e. strong) guidance in 2001 with a view to achieving greater consistency across local authorities.[59] The main points in the guidance are set out below, with some comment added. Further statutory guidance has been issued to local authorities suggesting how they should calculate charges as a percentage of an individual's personal budget (see Chapter 9).[60]

No presumption of charging

The guidance states that it makes no presumption that local authorities will charge for non-residential social services, since the 1983 Act creates only a power, not a duty. Therefore, local authorities retain substantial discretion in determining local policy, so long as it is consistent with the objectives in the guidance.[61]

Avoid impoverishing people

The guidance states that local authorities should not charge people who are on a level of income equal to basic levels of income support plus 25 per cent. For service users with higher income levels, charges should not be imposed that have the effect of reducing the person's income below those income support levels plus 25 per cent.[62]

Taking account of people's disability benefits as income

The guidance states that some disability benefits may be taken into account as income, namely the income support severe disability premium, attendance allowance, disability living allowance (DLA), constant attendance allowance, and exceptionally severe disablement allowance. War pensioners' mobility supplement and the mobility component of disability living allowance may not be taken into account[63] and likewise

58 Audit Commission (2000) *Charging with Care: How Councils Charge for Home Care.* London: AC.
59 Department of Health (2003) *Fairer Charging Policies* ... para 8.
60 Department of Health (2009) *Fairer Contributions Guidance: Calculating an Individual's Contribution to their Personal Budget.* London: DH, 2009.
61 Department of Health (2003) *Fairer Charging Policies* ... paras 4–5.
62 Department of Health (2003) *Fairer Charging Policies* ... para 20.
63 Department of Health (2003) *Fairer Charging Policies* ... paras 30–31.

age-related payments to pensioners under the Age Related Payments Act 2004.[64]

The fact that a person is receiving income from benefits does not necessarily mean that this income is disposable and can automatically be taken account of by local authorities in assessing charges. There may be a significant discrepancy between maximum state benefits payable and expenditure reasonably incurred by disabled people. A 2004 report concluded that, for 'high to medium' needs, the weekly benefits payable amounted to £235, but that budgetary requirements (excluding personal assistance) were £467, resulting in a weekly shortfall of £232.[65]

Assessing people's disability-related expenditure before deciding what they can afford to pay

The guidance states that if disability benefits are taken into account, the person must not be left without the means to pay for other necessary care and support or for other costs arising from their disability. Therefore, local authorities should specifically assess the disability-related expenditure of any service user.[66]

The guidance gives a non-exhaustive list of items of disability-related expenditure including community alarm systems, privately arranged care, specialist washing powders or laundry, special dietary needs, special clothing or footwear, additional bedding (e.g. because of incontinence), additional heating, domestic assistance (maintenance, cleaning, etc.) required because of the disability, disability-related equipment (e.g. purchase, maintenance, repair, hire), and transport costs over and above the mobility component of DLA.[67]

In practice, the approach of some local authorities appears rough, ready and harsh. However, this may have legal consequences. For instance, one local authority took an unlawfully restrictive approach to recognising payments – made to other family members for providing assistance – as legitimate disability-related expenditure.[68] Another took a blanket approach in excluding holiday expenditure from consideration and similarly lost a legal challenge.[69]

---

64 LAC (2004)25. Department of Health. *Charges for Residential Accommodation – CRAG Amendment No. 22.* London: DH.

65 Smith, N., Middleton, S., Ashton-Brooks, K., Cos, L., Dobson, B. and Reith, L. (2004) *Disabled People's Costs of Living: More Than You Would Think.* York: Joseph Rowntree Foundation, p.77.

66 Department of Health (2003) *Fairer Charging Policies ...* para 33.

67 Department of Health (2003) *Fairer Charging Policies ...* para 46.

68 *R(Stephenson) v Stockton-on-Tees Borough Council* [2005] EWCA Civ 960, Court of Appeal.

69 *R(B) v Cornwall County Council* [2009] EWHC 491 (Admin).

Day and night services

The guidance states that when assessing a charge for daytime services, local authorities should avoid taking account of, as income, the element of benefits that are payable for night care (the courts have held such practice to be irrational).[70] Normally it would be reasonable to treat the difference between DLA care component high rate and middle rate as representing the element paid for night care.[71]

Taking account of people's capital assets

The guidance states that service users with savings over the upper threshold figure used to assess charges for residential care (see Chapter 5) may be asked to pay the full cost of a non-residential service. But in assessing capital, the person's home should be disregarded.[72]

Personal-injury compensation payments

Local authorities often question if they can take account of personal-injury compensation payments. Department of Health guidance[73] states that the same approach to capital resources should be taken for non-residential charges as for residential accommodation charges (see Chapter 5). So the courts have stated that trust-held or court-held injury compensation capital sums cannot be taken into account for non-residential services. But because the guidance does not state that income from such capital sums should be treated in the same way as for residential accommodation, the local authority would retain discretion to take account of such income for non-residential services.[74]

Whose resources can be taken into account?

Under the legislation,[75] only the service user's means may be assessed, not those of other members of the family. However, the guidance suggests that in some circumstances the service user may have a legal right to share in the value of an asset, even if the asset is not in his or her name. This may be through statutory or equitable rights.[76]

Disregarding earnings

The guidance states that all earnings should be disregarded as income. This is so that a disincentive to work is not created.[77]

---

70 R(Carton) v Coventry City Council (2001) 4 CCLR 41.

71 Department of Health (2003) Fairer Charging Policies ... paras 35–43.

72 Department of Health (2003) Fairer Charging Policies ... paras 58–59.

73 Department of Health (2003) Fairer Charging Policies ... para 59.

74 Crofton v NHS Litigation Authority [2007] EWCA Civ 71.

75 Health and Social Services and Social Security Adjudications Act 1983, s.17.

76 Department of Health (2003) Fairer Charging Policies ... para 64.

77 Department of Health (2003) Fairer Charging Policies ... para 72.

Full cost of the service

The guidance states that the maximum charge must not exceed the full cost of providing the service. It should not include costs associated with the purchasing function or costs of operating the charging system. If the costs of services vary within a local authority's area (e.g. because of diverse provider charges), it is for the local authority to decide whether to set a notional average (e.g. to avoid people in rural areas being disadvantaged).[78]

Carers

The guidance states that if informal carers are being charged for carers' services under the Carers and Disabled Children Act 2000, then the local authority should take account of costs that the carers may be incurring, before deciding what to charge. For example, private purchase of care (to allow short breaks), adaptations to the carer's home (e.g. where the disabled person has moved in), additional transport costs (e.g. taxis because there is not time to use public transport), and additional costs relating to the person's disability that the carer meets.[79]

Direct payments

The guidance states that direct payment recipients are to be charged in the same way as if they had received the equivalent services from the local authority.[80]

NHS payments

The guidance states that if a person's community care services are being in effect paid for by NHS money, transferred to the local authority via the NHS Act 2006, service users could still be charged up to the full cost of the service.[81]

Refusal to pay charge

The guidance states that a service should not be withdrawn because a person refuses to pay a charge; however, the debt could be pursued through the civil courts.[82]

The local ombudsman has questioned the dividing line between a person declining services (in reaction to charges being imposed), and the local authority withdrawing services – particularly when both staff and service user are ignorant of the legal position. So, it was

---

78 Department of Health (2003) *Fairer Charging Policies* ... paras 77, 79.
79 Department of Health (2003) *Fairer Charging Policies* ... para 83.
80 Department of Health (2003) *Fairer Charging Policies* ... para 86.
81 Department of Health (2003) *Fairer Charging Policies* ... para 88.
82 Department of Health (2003) *Fairer Charging Policies* ... para 97.

maladministration when local authority staff had not explained about the continuing duty to provide services even if a person did not pay; the man had suspended the care being provided for his wife, because he was having difficulty meeting the charges.[83]

Refusal to disclose resources
The guidance states that if people refuse to disclose their resources, it may be reasonable to charge them the full cost of the service.[84]

Consultation about charges
The guidance states that changes to charging policies, including increases, should be consulted on with users and carers.[85]

The courts have confirmed that when a local authority is making fundamental changes to its charging system, fairness requires that proper consultation take place.[86] For instance, a mere six weeks of consultation, and then with too small a group of local representatives, meant the local authority was inadequately informed about the concerns of local voluntary bodies.[87] The local ombudsman has stated that introducing a charging system from scratch requires consultation.[88] Furthermore, a local authority should not conceal crucial detail from the consultation – for example, the fact that it wanted to raise charges from £1 to £46 a day.[89]

Scope of review in considering reasonable practicability of person paying the assessed charge
Guidance states that fairness of the charge should be considered in the light of individual circumstances. Any review may need to go beyond consideration of the terms of the council's policy, since the policy is unlikely to make provision for all conceivable personal circumstances.[90]

---

83 *Durham County Council 2000* (99/C/1983).
84 Department of Health (2003) *Fairer Charging Policies* ... para 97.
85 Department of Health (2003) *Fairer Charging Policies* ... para 98.
86 *R(Carton) v Coventry City Council* (2001) 4 CCLR 41.
87 *R(Berry) v Cumbria County Council* [2007] EWHC Admin 3144.
88 *Derbyshire County Council 2004* (02/C/14235 and others).
89 *Oldham Metropolitan Borough Council 2007* (05/C/08648).
90 Department of Health (2003) *Fairer Charging Policies* ... para 101.

CHAPTER 7

Informal carers

- Right of informal carer to have an assessment
  - Carer's assessment in its own right
  - Request for an assessment
  - Informal carer: definition
  - Carer providing substantial care on a regular basis
  - Assessment of ability to care
  - Right of informal carer to be had regard to
- Services for carers
  - Range of carers' services
  - Services for the carer or the cared-for person?
  - Direct payments for carers
- Other legislation affecting carers

SUMMARY

At least six pieces of legislation are directly relevant to informal carers. These are the Carers (Equal Opportunities) Act 2004, Carers and Disabled Children Act 2000, Carers (Recognition and Services) Act 1995, Children Act 1989 (s.17), Disabled Persons (Services, Consultation and Representation) Act 1986 (s.8) and the NHS Act 2006 (s.254 and schedule 20).

This legislation is important because informal carers (largely families but others as well) shoulder substantial caring burdens. If assistance is not provided, breaking point, physically and emotionally, can soon be reached with the endless pressure of care – including sleep deprivation, moving and handling and being the only person who can provide what is needed.[1]

---

1   MENCAP (2006) *Breaking Point: Families Still Need a Break.* London: MENCAP.

RIGHT OF INFORMAL CARER TO HAVE AN ASSESSMENT

Under the Carers (Recognition and Services) Act 1995 and the Carers and Disabled Children Act 2000, informal carers are entitled, if certain conditions are met, to have their ability to care assessed by local authorities.

Under the 1995 Act, for an informal carer to be entitled to an assessment, the local authority must be carrying out a community care assessment of the person cared for under s.47 of the NHS and Community Care Act 1990. In the case of a disabled child, there must be an assessment of that child under Part 3 of the Children Act 1989 or s.2 of the Chronically Sick and Disabled Persons Act 1970.

CARER'S ASSESSMENT IN ITS OWN RIGHT

Under the 2000 Act, in contrast to the 1995 Act, a carer's assessment is an entitlement irrespective of whether an assessment of the person cared for has taken place. The condition for a carer's assessment is simply that he or she must be caring for a person for whom the local authority is satisfied that it has the power to provide or arrange community care services. The cared-for person must be must be at least 18 years old, the carer at least 16 years old. In the case of a parent of a disabled child, the local authority must be satisfied that it has the power to provide or arrange services for the child and family under s.17 of the Children Act 1989.

The carer could be entitled to an assessment, even if the cared-for person has been assessed as not being eligible for community care services because his or her needs are deemed too low. This is because even a cared-for person with 'low' needs is still a person for whom the local authority *may* provide community services. It is just that it has chosen not to do so.

(Any informal carer, aged 16 years or over, is potentially entitled to an assessment under the 1995 or the 2000 Acts. Less than 16 years old, as a young carer, he or she would be entitled to an assessment under the 1995 Act only. However, such a child might also have a right to be assessed as a child in need under s.17 of the Children Act 1989.)

REQUEST FOR AN ASSESSMENT

The carer must make a request before the duty to assess is triggered. Arguably it is the substance of a request, rather than the formality, that counts.[2] The local ombudsman has found local authorities failing to tell carers of their right to an assessment,[3] and avoiding carers' assessments.[4] In the light of such failings, the Carers (Equal Opportunities) Act 2004 amended both the 1995 and the 2000 Acts. The local authority must now inform carers about their right to request an assessment.

INFORMAL CARER: DEFINITION
Under both the 1995 and 2000 Acts, the definition of carer excludes both paid carers and volunteers from a voluntary organisation.

CARER PROVIDING SUBSTANTIAL CARE ON A REGULAR BASIS
The duty of a local authority to assess a carer arises only if substantial care on a regular basis is involved.

Department of Health policy guidance states that local authorities should judge substantial and regular care in relation to the overall impact on the carer of the whole caring situation. Caring might not necessarily be founded on physical tasks, and it might be periodic, sporadic or preventative in nature; and it might involve anxiety or stress. Caring responsibilities may conflict with either family or work responsibilities.[5]

The approach of the guidance means that an over-simple criterion, such as the number of hours spent each week on the caring role, should not be decisive.

ASSESSMENT OF ABILITY TO CARE
Assessment under both 1995 and 2000 Acts must be of a carer's ability to care. The Carers (Equal Opportunities) Act 2004 extended this to consideration also of whether the carer is engaging in, or wishes to engage, in work, training, education, leisure. This is a reminder that carers have lives as well.

RIGHT OF INFORMAL CARER TO BE HAD REGARD TO
If an informal carer of a disabled person does not wish for an assessment, or does not request it, the local authority is still obliged to take account

2 *R v Bexley London Borough Council, ex p B* [1995] CL 3225.
3 *North Yorkshire County Council 2002* (01/C/03521).
4 *Salford City Council 2003* (01/C/17519).
5 Department of Health (2005) *Carers and Disabled Children Act 2000 and Carers (Equal Opportunities) Act 2004 Combined Policy Guidance.* London: DH, p.22.

of that carer's ability to care when deciding what welfare services to provide for the disabled person.[6]

SERVICES FOR CARERS

Under the Carers and Disabled Children Act 2000, where the cared-for person is 18 years or over, a local authority has a duty to consider:

(a) whether the carer has needs in relation to the care being or intended to be provided

(b) whether those needs could be satisfied wholly or in part by services that the local authority has the power to provide, and if so

(c) whether or not to provide these services.

This threefold duty is expressed tortuously; it apparently creates a duty to decide whether to provide services but no duty actually to provide them. Even so, a local authority cannot simply choose never to provide services. It has to decide in each case. Never to provide would unlawfully fetter its discretion.[7]

The power to provide services in the 2000 Act applies only in the case of carers aged at least 16 years old, who are caring for a person 18 years old or over. For parents (as carers) of disabled children, services would fall to be provided under s.17 of the Children Act 1989.

RANGE OF CARERS' SERVICES

If provision of carers' services seems legally to entail a power rather than a duty, nonetheless there is a potential strength. The services that can be provided are not defined, and so can be wide ranging. Examples from Department of Health practice guidance include shopping, cleaning, a washing machine in the informal carer's own home (to deal with incontinence laundry), a travel warrant for the brother of a person with a psychotic illness to come and stay for a week (thus giving the mother a break), and trips to art galleries (for a 17-year-old carer to get a break while caring for his dying father).[8] Policy guidance states that

---

6   *Disabled Persons (Services, Consultation and Representation) Act 1986*, s.8.

7   *British Oxygen v Board of Trade* [1971] AC 610, House of Lords.

8   Department of Health (2001) *Carers and People with Parental Responsibility for Disabled Children: Practice Guidance.* London: DH, paras 80–102.

services 'may take any form' – for example, a gardening service – and that practitioners are encouraged to be flexible and innovative.[9]

SERVICES FOR THE CARER OR THE CARED-FOR PERSON?

Some services could be characterised as either being for the disabled person or for the carer – for instance, a laundry service. However, carers' services are not allowed to include anything of an intimate nature in respect of the person being cared for.

There are exceptions to this intimacy rule. During the delivery of what is meant to be a non-intimate service, the paid carer may deliver an intimate service (a) if the person providing the service is asked by the cared-for person, (b) if the person lacks capacity to consent to such a service but it is provided in accordance with the principles of the Mental Capacity Act 2005, or (c) if the person cared for is otherwise likely, imminently, to suffer serious personal harm.[10]

Guidance states that a service of an intimate nature involves:

(a) lifting, washing, grooming, feeding, dressing, bathing, toileting, medicine administration, or other forms of physical contact

(b) assistance in connection with washing, grooming, feeding, dressing, bathing, administering medicines or using the toilet

(c) supervision of the person while he or she is dressing, bathing or using the toilet. The overall purpose of the rule is to 'prevent any services being delivered to unwilling disabled or frail people.[11]

DIRECT PAYMENTS FOR CARERS

Where the local authority has decided to provide a carer's service, the service could be directly provided or a direct payment made.[12]

OTHER LEGISLATION AFFECTING CARERS

Services for informal carers are potentially available under at least three pieces of legislation other than the 1986, 1995 and 2000 Acts dealt with above. The first is the Children Act 1989, s.17. This contains a

---

9 Department of Health (2005) *Carers and Disabled Children Act 2000 and Carers (Equal Opportunities) Act 2004 Combined Policy Guidance.* London: DH, para 52.

10 SI 2001/441. *Carers (Services) and Direct Payments (Amendment) (England) Regulations 2001.*

11 Department of Health (2005) *Carers and Disabled Children Act 2000* ... paras 56–57.

12 *Health and Social Care Act 2001,* s.57; *Children Act 1989,* s.17A; SI 2009/1887. *The Community Care, Services for Carers and Children's Services (Direct Payments) (England) Regulations 2009.*

general duty to safeguard and promote the welfare of children in need by provision of services not only for the children but also for other family members.

The second is s.254 and schedule 20 of the NHS Act 2006. These place on local authorities a general duty to provide, for 'households', home help and a power to provide laundry facilities (see Chapter 6). The duty would appear not to exclude provision for informal carers.

Third, the Carers (Equal Opportunities) Act 2004 imposes a duty on other bodies, including other social services authorities, housing authorities, education authorities and NHS bodies. A local authority can ask any of these to assist with both assessment and the provision of services; the body requested must give due consideration to the request. This means there is no duty to comply with the request, just so long as it is not ignored.[13]

Last, the NHS Act 2006, in terms of NHS provision, does not explicitly refer to carers at all. However, there would appear to be nothing to stop the NHS making plentiful provision for carers. For instance, under schedule 3 of the NHS Act 2006, a PCT can do anything appearing to it to be necessary or expedient in relation to its functions.

---

13 Department of Health (2005) *Carers and Disabled Children Act 2000* ... para 36.

CHAPTER 8

Direct payments: giving people money

- Direct payments: duty and power
  - Duty to make a direct payment
  - Power to make a direct payment
  - Prohibition on direct payments
- Consent and ability to manage a direct payment
  - Needs calling for services
  - Consent to a direct payment
  - Ability to manage the payment
- People lacking capacity to consent to a direct payment
  - Consent in relation to a person lacking capacity
  - Suitability of somebody else to receive the direct payment
  - Conditions to be met before payment is made for person lacking capacity
  - Further rules about the direct payment made to a suitable person
- Services for which direct payments are available
- Direct payments and close relatives
- Amount of direct payment
- Charging and direct payments
- Community equipment and direct payments
- Health and safety, and safeguarding
- Imposing conditions on direct payments
- Monitoring and reviewing direct payments
- Withdrawing or withholding a direct payment
- Third party or indirect payments
- Direct payments from the NHS
- Vouchers
- Independent Living Fund

SUMMARY

If certain conditions are met, local authorities have a duty to make direct payments of money to people. This is so people can buy their own community care services – rather than have the local authority provide or arrange them. The stated purpose of direct payments is to give service users greater independence and control over their daily lives. Direct payments are part of a wider policy of personalisation or self-directed support; this is discussed in the next chapter. It is intended that in the future direct payments should be extended to the NHS.

Overall, direct payments are about giving people greater choice and control over how their needs are met. The principle is sound but two major question marks remain. The first is whether local authorities will in future make adequate levels of payment to enable people to buy what they need. The second is whether local authorities will provide adequate support for people, particularly those who are more vulnerable, in order to facilitate this exercise of choice and control – and, where necessary, safeguard them from abuse or neglect.

This chapter also makes brief mention of two policies related to direct payments: the social-care voucher scheme and also the Independent Living Fund.

DIRECT PAYMENTS: DUTY AND POWER

A number of different groups of people are eligible to receive direct payments. In most cases, if certain conditions are met, a local authority comes under a duty to make a direct payment. In some cases, there is a power only; there are also a few prohibitions. The rules are reasonably clear but it is not uncommon for local authorities to fail to spell them out to people; not to do so, however, may be maladministration.[1] Local authorities may simply not offer direct payments to certain groups of people even where there is a duty to do so; this, too, is maladministration[2] and potentially unlawful.

DUTY TO MAKE A DIRECT PAYMENT

A duty applies potentially to the following groups, assuming other requisite conditions are satisfied. First, to community-care service users

---

1   *Ealing London Borough Council 2008* (06/A/08746).
2   *Kent County Council 2009* (08/005/002).

aged 18 or over with an assessed eligible need under s.47 of the NHS and Community Care Act 1990. Second, to informal carers (aged 16 or over), for whom the local authority has decided services are called for. Third, to those people who lack capacity to consent to direct payments. Last, to the parents of disabled children, disabled parents of children, and children aged 16 or 17 years old; in each of these cases, the child concerned must be a child in need under s.17 of the Children Act 1989, for whose needs the local authority has decided services are called for.[3]

POWER TO MAKE A DIRECT PAYMENT

A power applies to people who, under certain mental health or criminal justice legislation, are under an obligation to receive services (which could, however, be provided through direct payments).

Note. The provisions covered are supervision orders under the Criminal Procedure (Insanity) Act 1964 (schedule 1, Part 1); guardianship under the Mental Health Act 1983 (s.8, s.40(2)); community treatment orders under the Mental Health Act 1983 (17B); mental-health treatment requirement under the Criminal Justice Act 2003 (s.177, s.189, s.207); mental health requirement under the Powers of Criminal Courts (Sentencing) Act 2000 (s.41, s.51); mental health treatment under the Criminal Justice Act 1991 (s.37(4)); and also various similar Scottish legislation).[4]

PROHIBITION ON DIRECT PAYMENTS

Some people are excluded altogether from direct payments. These are people subject to a drug rehabilitation requirement,[5] to an alcohol treatment requirement (imposed by community order or suspended sentence of imprisonment);[6] to drug or alcohol dependency treatment;[7] to a drug treatment and testing order (and similar under Scottish legislation).[8]

CONSENT AND ABILITY TO MANAGE A DIRECT PAYMENT

For a duty or a power to arise, certain conditions must be met.

---

3   *Health and Social Care Act 2001*, s.57; *Children Act 1989*, s.17A; SI 2009/1887. *The Community Care, Services for Carers and Children's Services (Direct Payments) (England) Regulations 2009.*

4   SI 2009/1887. SI 2009/1887. *The Community Care, Services for Carers and Children's Services (Direct Payments) (England) Regulations 2009*, schedule 2.

5   *Criminal Justice Act 2003*, s.209.

6   *Criminal Justice Act 2003*, s.212.

7   *Powers of Criminal Courts (Sentencing) Act 2000*, s.41 (rehabilitation order) or s.51 (community punishment and rehabilitation order).

8   *Powers of the Criminal Courts (Sentencing) Act 2000*, s.52.

NEEDS CALLING FOR SERVICES

First, there must be an assessed need calling for services. A person's needs could be met in part by the making of a direct payment, and in part by directly provided services arranged by the local authority.[9] It need not be all or nothing.

CONSENT TO A DIRECT PAYMENT

Second, the recipient of the direct payment must also consent.[10] This implies the need for both mental capacity and willingness; the ombudsman has pointed out that direct payments should not be forced on people;[11] statutory guidance states the same.[12] Even so, the courts have held that if a person refuses a direct payment, the speed with which the local authority must provide an alternative may depend on the reasonableness of the person's refusal.[13] The need for consent applies both to the service user with mental capacity, and to a suitable person acting as recipient on behalf of a service user lacking capacity.

ABILITY TO MANAGE THE PAYMENT

Third, the recipient must be able to manage the payment with or without assistance.[14] Guidance states that ability to manage must not be confused with capacity to consent. The following should be considered:

(a) the person's understanding of direct payments (and what is required of the person)

(b) the implications of taking or not taking on direct payments

(c) available help

(d) what support would be needed

(e) what arrangements the person would have to make to obtain this support.[15]

The guidance states that such assistance could include, for example, keeping records, management of day-to-day relationships with staff

---

9 Department of Health (2009) *Guidance on Direct Payments for Community Care, Services for Carers and Children's Services*. London: DH, para 28.

10 *Health and Social Care Act 2001*, s.57; *Children Act 1989*, s.17A.

11 *Cambridgeshire County Council 2002* (01/B/00305).

12 Department of Health (2009) *Guidance on Direct Payments for Community Care* … para 15.

13 *R(P) v Hackney London Borough Council* [2007] EWHC 1365 Admin.

14 SI 2009/1887. *The Community Care, Services* … rr.2, 8.

15 Department of Health (2009) *Guidance on Direct Payments for Community Care* … paras 66–71.

or using a payroll service; the assistance itself might be bought in.[16] Thus, the ombudsman found maladministration when a local authority refused to make a direct payment just because a woman with learning disabilities could not manage without assistance.[17]

PEOPLE LACKING CAPACITY TO CONSENT TO A DIRECT PAYMENT

Special, additional, rules apply to people lacking capacity to consent to a direct payment. If certain conditions are met, they place a duty on the local authority to make a direct payment to somebody else – in effect, an alternative recipient. There are three key issues. First, requisite consent must be given; second the recipient must be suitable; third, the local authority must be satisfied that it is appropriate to make the payment. These represent an attempt by central government to strike a middle path – by extending the flexibility of direct payments to people lacking capacity, while at the same time retaining a number of safeguards.

CONSENT IN RELATION TO A PERSON LACKING CAPACITY

As to consent, the alternative recipient of the payment must in any event give consent. If there is a 'surrogate' for the person lacking capacity, and the surrogate is not going to be the recipient of the direct payment, then that surrogate has to consent as well. A surrogate is defined as either a deputy appointed by the Court of Protection under the Mental Capacity Act 2005, or the 'donee' of a lasting power of attorney made under the same Act – either of whose role is defined to include powers relevant to community care services.[18]

SUITABILITY OF SOMEBODY ELSE TO RECEIVE THE DIRECT PAYMENT

The recipient of the direct payment is automatically suitable if he or she is a representative of the person lacking capacity. A representative is defined as a person with a lasting power of attorney or a deputy appointed by the Court of Protection. If the proposed recipient is not a representative of the person, he or she might still be suitable but only if both the local authority and any surrogate consider this to be so. If

16 Department of Health (2009) *Guidance on Direct Payments for Community Care* ... para 74.
17 *Hertfordshire County Council 2003* (01/B/09360).
18 SI 2009/1887. *The Community Care, Services* ... r.6.

there is no surrogate, then the local authority alone has to consider whether the proposed recipient is suitable.[19]

CONDITIONS TO BE MET BEFORE PAYMENT IS MADE FOR PERSON LACKING CAPACITY

Before deciding, overall, whether to make the direct payment to a suitable person, the local authority must take certain steps. First, as far as is reasonably practicable and appropriate, it must consult with:

(a) anyone named by the person lacking capacity who should be consulted with

(b) anyone engaged in caring for the person or interested in their welfare, and

(c) any surrogate or representative.

Second, as far as is reasonably practicable it must consider the person's past and present wishes and feelings (and in particular any written statement made before capacity was lost), the person's beliefs and values, and any other factors the person would have considered had capacity been retained.

Third, the authority must obtain an enhanced criminal record certificate, where the proposed recipient of the direct payment is not (a) a partner or spouse, (b) a close relative living in the same household, or (c) a friend involved in the provision of care for the person lacking capacity.

Fourth, overall, the local authority must be satisfied that the person's needs will be met by the direct payment, the recipient will act in the best interests of the person lacking capacity, the recipient can manage the payment with or without assistance, and in all the circumstances it is appropriate for the payment to be made.[20]

FURTHER RULES ABOUT THE DIRECT PAYMENT MADE TO A SUITABLE PERSON

The suitable person must (a) act in the best interests of the person lacking capacity, (b) provide information the local authority requests, (c) tell the local authority if the person lacking capacity no longer lacks capacity,

---

19 *Health and Social Care Act 2001*, s.57(1C).
20 SI 2009/1887. *The Community Care, Services ... r.8.*

(d) use the payment to obtain the services for which the payment was agreed.[21]

In addition, if the suitable person is not a spouse, partner or close relative or the person lacking capacity, then he or she must obtain a criminal record certificate in respect of anybody being paid to provide the service. In these circumstances, the suitable person is defined as a 'regulated activity provider' under the Safeguarding Vulnerable Groups Act 2006.[22]

SERVICES FOR WHICH DIRECT PAYMENTS ARE AVAILABLE

Direct payments are available for non-residential services including community equipment. They may, however, be used for residential accommodation (i.e. a care home) but only if the accommodation is provided for no more than four continuous weeks in any period of 12 months. Shorter stays are to be added together, unless they are separated by a period of four weeks or more. However, they must anyway not exceed 120 days a year.[23]

In one case, the court accepted that the placement of a child in a residential educational establishment involved the provision of a significant amount of social care and practical assistance, which did not amount to provision of residential accommodation. Therefore, direct payments were legally available for this element of the child's needs.[24] The same principle applies to adults, as confirmed by statutory guidance – for instance, a care home resident using direct payments for daytime activities.[25]

DIRECT PAYMENTS AND CLOSE RELATIVES

A direct payment may not be used to pay a spouse or partner or other close relatives living in the same household, unless this is necessary in order for the needs of the person to be met satisfactorily – or, in respect of a child-related direct payment, it is necessary for promoting the welfare of the child. The list of relatives comprises parent or parent-in-law, son or daughter, son-in-law or daughter-in-law, stepson or stepdaughter, brother or sister, aunt or uncle, grandparent, spouse, or any person

---

21 SI 2009/1887. *The Community Care, Services* ... r.12.
22 Department of Health (2009) *Guidance on Direct Payments for Community Care* ... paras 153–155.
23 SI 2009/1887. *The Community Care, Services* ... r.13.
24 *R(M) v Suffolk County Council* [2006] EWHC 2366 Admin.
25 Department of Health (2009) *Guidance on Direct Payments for Community Care* ... para 106.

living as spouse with anybody on this list.[26] In the case of a person lacking capacity, guidance states that payment by the suitable person of such a spouse, partner or family member should be exceptional.[27]

AMOUNT OF DIRECT PAYMENT

The local authority must make the payment at a rate that it estimates 'to be equivalent to the reasonable cost of securing the provision of the service concerned'.[28] Department of Health guidance emphasises that the payment should be sufficient to enable the recipient 'lawfully to secure the service of a standard that the council considers is reasonable to fulfil the relevant needs'. There should be 'no limit on the maximum or minimum amount' of the amount of care to be purchased, or of the value of the direct payment.[29]

Therefore, financial ceilings imposed irrespective of individual circumstances and as a matter of policy – for example, on the total weekly amount, or on the hourly rate that the direct payment will cover – are likely to be unlawful. Such ceilings would also risk unlawfully fettering the local authority's discretion if applied in blanket fashion. For instance, the local ombudsman criticised a ceiling of £360 per week offered by way of direct payment, to pay for two evening carers for a woman; that amount was insufficient for the purpose of meeting her assessed needs.[30]

Guidance also states that the direct payment might also need to include an amount to cover recruitment costs, National Insurance, statutory holiday pay, sick pay, maternity pay, employers' liability insurance, public liability insurance and VAT.[31] In this vein, the courts accepted in one case that the reasonable cost of the direct payment should include insurance to cover liability for injury caused to the service provider by the service user, or possibly an indemnity against any such liability. It also needed to include provision for income tax and National Insurance payments.[32]

26 SI 2009/1887. *The Community Care, Services* ... rr.11–12.

27 Department of Health (2009) *Guidance on Direct Payments for Community Care* ... paras 135, 197.

28 *Health and Social Care Act 2001*, s.57.

29 Department of Health (2009) *Guidance on Direct Payments for Community Care* ... para 111.

30 *Cambridgeshire County Council 2002* (01/B/00305).

31 Department of Health (2009) *Guidance on Direct Payments for Community Care* ... para 114.

32 *R(P) v Hackney London Borough Council* [2007] EWHC 1365 Admin.

CHARGING AND DIRECT PAYMENTS

A direct payment should be made gross, unless the local authority decides to make it net. So, it can reduce the payment if is satisfied that it is reasonably practicable for the recipient to contribute towards the cost of the service. Alternatively, even where this is reasonably practicable, the local authority can still make the gross payment, but then demand payment of the assessed contribution.[33]

COMMUNITY EQUIPMENT AND DIRECT PAYMENTS

Department of Health guidance makes clear that direct payments apply to equipment, as well as to other community care services. It states that the recipient should be supported by adequate expertise, especially where major items of equipment are concerned. The local authority should also clarify responsibilities for ongoing care and maintenance, as well as what should happen when the person no longer needs the equipment.[34]

HEALTH AND SAFETY, AND SAFEGUARDING

Some local authorities express concerns over health and safety issues in the context of direct payments. Department of Health guidance states that as 'a general principle, local councils should avoid laying down health and safety policies for individual direct payment recipients'. However, local authorities should give people information and risk assessments about health and safety.[35]

This guidance represents a hands-off approach. It is consistent with the purpose of direct payments – to give disabled people more control and responsibility. Some local authorities believe this approach will protect them from negligence liability in case of accident; however, other authorities are more nervous about stepping back too far.

Guidance states that, in the case of service users with capacity, local authorities should inform them about the option of having a Criminal Records Bureau check done on somebody being employed. The choice of whether to do so is the recipient's.[36] For people who lack capacity, there are particular rules about this (set out earlier in this chapter).

---

33 *Health and Social Care Act 2001*, s.57; SI 2009/1887. *The Community Care, Services* ... r.10.

34 Department of Health (2009) *Guidance on Direct Payments for Community Care* ... paras 107–110.

35 Department of Health (2009) *Guidance on Direct Payments for Community Care* ... paras 132–134.

36 Department of Health (2009) *Guidance on Direct Payments for Community Care* ... para 129.

IMPOSING CONDITIONS ON DIRECT PAYMENTS

The local authority can attach conditions to a direct payment; these can include that the payment not be used to purchase services from a particular named person and that the recipient provide information about use of the direct payment.[37] Guidance states that local authorities 'may set reasonable conditions on the direct payment, but need to bear in mind when doing so that the aim of a direct payment is to give people more choice and control ... Conditions should be proportionate'. Thus, conditions should not be imposed limiting the choice of provider the person could use.[38]

MONITORING AND REVIEWING DIRECT PAYMENTS

The guidance states that monitoring of a direct payment should be proportionate.[39] As to review, it states that this, too, should be proportionate and could be 'light touch', less frequent and on the telephone – or more frequent and face to face. It states that reviews should be carried out according to existing guidance on 'fair access to care'[40] (although the guidance referred to states that only exceptionally should review be other than face to face).[41] In the case of people lacking capacity, regulations state that there must be a review within the first year, and at least annually thereafter.[42] Guidance concedes it might need to be more frequent.[43]

WITHDRAWING OR WITHHOLDING A DIRECT PAYMENT

A local authority may withdraw a direct payment if specified conditions are no longer satisfied – for example, if the person's needs are no longer being met. Nevertheless, if a person is unable, temporarily, to manage the payment, the local authority can continue to make the payment if somebody else is prepared to accept and manage it, and the service provider agrees to accept payment from that other person.[44]

---

37 SI 2009/1887. *The Community Care, Services* ... rr.11–12.
38 Department of Health (2009) *Guidance on Direct Payments for Community Care* ... para 92.
39 Department of Health (2009) *Guidance on Direct Payments for Community Care* ... para 226.
40 Department of Health (2009) *Guidance on Direct Payments for Community Care* ... paras 131, 226.
41 LAC(2002)13. Department of Health. *Fair Access to Care Services: Guidance on Eligibility Criteria for Adult Social Care.* London: DH.
42 SI 2009/1887. *The Community Care, Services* ... rr.16.
43 Department of Health (2009) *Guidance on Direct Payments for Community Care* ... para 228.
44 SI 2009/1887. *The Community Care, Services* .... r.17.

The legislation also allows the local authority to seek repayment if the money has not been used to secure a relevant service or if a condition of the direct payment agreement has been breached.[45] Department of Health guidance states that this power to recover money should not be used either to penalise honest mistakes, or to seek repayment where the recipient has been the victim of fraud.[46]

THIRD PARTY OR INDIRECT PAYMENTS

Until November 2009, it was not legally possible to make a direct payment to a person who lacked the capacity to consent to it. Nor was it possible to make the direct payment to anybody else (other than parents in the case of children). This did not stop some local authorities breaking the rules, tempted to do so because of direct payment targets set by central government.

However, there was, and still is, an alternative. For instance, the courts have held that, in the case of mental incapacity, a local authority has a legal power (though not a duty) to make a payment to a user independent trust (UIT) – which can administer the money flexibly after the fashion of a direct payment. This was established in a dispute about the manual handling of two adult sisters with learning disabilities – who lacked the capacity to receive a direct payment. The judge held that the payment could not be made to the parents under direct payments legislation. However, under s.30 of the National Assistance Act 1948 (or possibly s.2 of the Local Government Act 2000), the money could be paid to a UIT, which could in turn set up and manage the care package.[47]

DIRECT PAYMENTS FROM THE NHS

Direct payments legislation covers community care services only. It follows that, under it, the NHS cannot make direct payments for health care services.[48] However, central government intends that direct payments be extended to the NHS; the Health Act 2009 will make this possible.[49]

---

45 SI 2009/1887. *The Community Care, Services* ... r.15.
46 Department of Health (2009) *Guidance on Direct Payments for Community Care* ... para 245.
47 *R(A&B, X&Y) v East Sussex County Council* [2002] EWHC Admin 2771.
48 *R(Harrison) v Secretary of State for Health* [2009] EWHC 574 Admin.
49 Department of Health (2009) *Direct Payments for Health Care: Consultation on Proposals for Regulations and Guidance*. London: DH.

Note. The NHS may, under s.256 of the NHS Act 2006, make payments to local authorities to help the latter provide social services. This money could be used in the form of direct payments but not in respect of health care services, such as registered nursing care, which local authorities are not allowed to provide.[50] Alternatively, under s.75 of the 2006 Act, the NHS could give local authorities money for the latter to deliver health services on behalf of the NHS. But this would still not allow for direct payments because direct payments can only be made for community care services and not for health services. Nonetheless, NHS primary care trusts (PCTs) have, under their general powers, discretion to pay money to a user independent trust, a voluntary organisation or private care agency.[51] The money could then be used flexibly to arrange health care.[52]

VOUCHERS

The voucher system does not come under the direct payments legislation. Instead, local authorities have a legal power to issue vouchers for people to use flexibly in obtaining services from care providers. These can be issued in respect of an informal carer (at least 16 years old) of an adult, or for the parent of a disabled child – where it is agreed that a temporary break from caring would help.

Such breaks must last no longer than 28 days at any one time and cumulatively not exceed 120 days in any 12-month period. Vouchers may be expressed in terms of money or of time. A time voucher must specify the service for which it is valid; and it may, but does not have to, specify the supplier of services. Time vouchers may be issued either to the person cared for, or to the carer – if the cared-for person consents or lacks capacity to give that consent. In respect of children in need, they may be issued to the parent. However, money vouchers can be issued only to the person cared for or the parent of a child in need.[53]

A key difference between direct payments and vouchers is that, in the case of the former, the recipient of the payment takes on contractual responsibility; whereas with vouchers, the local authority retains that responsibility. Department of Health guidance states that a local authority's normal charging system for non-residential services should be applied to the provision of vouchers.[54]

---

50 *Health and Social Care Act 2001*, s.49; *National Assistance Act 1948*, s.29(6).

51 *NHS Act 2006*, s.12 and schedule 3, para 15.

52 *R(Gunter) v South Western Staffordshire Primary Care Trust* [2005] EWHC 1894 Admin; *R(Whapples) v Birmingham East Primary Care Trust* [2008] EWCA Civ 465.

53 *Carers and Disabled Children Act 2000*, s.3; *Children Act 1989*, s.17B; SI 2003/1216. *Carers and Disabled Children (Vouchers) (England) Regulations 2003.*

54 Department of Health (2003) *Carers and Disabled Children Act 2000: Vouchers for Short Term Breaks.* London: DH, paras 4–5, 25.

INDEPENDENT LIVING FUND

The Independent Living Fund is a quango attached to the Department of Work and Pensions. It provides grants for disabled people, to enable them to live in the community rather than in residential care. From October 2007, the two previous independent living funds ceased and were replaced by the Independent Living Fund (2006).[55] These grants obviously bear some similarity to direct payments.

In summary, the new Fund has the power 'to make payments to assist certain severely disabled people to live independently'. Various rules apply. A person must be under 65 years old on first application. In addition, a person must be receiving from the local authority services or direct payments to the value of a threshold sum of £320 per week. The Fund can pay the money to a third party to administer it, usually where the disabled person is unable to manage his or her own money. The 2006 Fund is primarily intended to pay for the cost of employing personal assistants to provide personal and domestic help. The money cannot be used to employ or pay close relatives living in the same household. There is also a range of services on which the money cannot be spent, including holidays, care homes, wheelchairs, equipment, home adaptations, furniture, physiotherapy, etc.[56]

---

55 *Disability (Grants) Act 1993*, s.1.
56 Secretary of State for Work and Pensions (2009) *Independent Living Fund: Trust Deed*. London: DWP.

CHAPTER 9

Personalisation and safeguarding adults

- Key elements of personalisation
  - Legal issues arising from personalisation
  - Self-assessment and general outcomes
  - Resource allocation systems and personal budgets
  - People's eligibility for personal budgets
- Safeguarding adults

SUMMARY
At the time of writing, there are two policies in particular affecting community care. The first is called 'personalisation' or self-directed support. The second is safeguarding adults, a term that has superseded adult protection in England (though not in Scotland). Neither is yet underpinned by legislation. Given how important both are in terms of people's fundamental welfare, this is a curious and certainly questionable state of affairs. Apart from creating uncertainty, it means that both policies have so far escaped the scrutiny, debate and (one hopes) logic that legislation brings.

PERSONALISATION
The key elements of personalisation are legally undefined, which creates uncertainty in practice. However, it needs to be covered in this book because, with or without explicit legislation and detailed guidance, local authorities are going ahead with the policy in any case. They are doing this at the bidding of central government, which has made clear that personalisation represents a major change to the way in which social care is provided. The idea is to give people

more choice, control, power and independence through a system of personal budgets. This is to replace what central government sees as the paternalistic, reactive care of the past with enablement and high-quality personally tailored services.[1]

Nevertheless, personalisation is, even in its early days, emerging as a two-faced policy, of the type referred to in Chapter 2. Looked at from one point of view, it is a welcome counterbalance to the excessive rigidity, bureaucracy and restrictions that have sometimes characterised local authority assessment and provision of community care. But looked at from another, the policy is likely to be used surreptitiously as a cost-cutting measure; this will lead inevitably to shortcuts, which will (a) undermine the principle of the new policy, (b) leave more vulnerable people to their own devices, and (c) in some instances risk being unlawful.

SAFEGUARDING ADULTS
The second key policy is called safeguarding adults, or 'adult protection'. This involves local authorities attempting to protect vulnerable adults from suffering significant harm in terms of abuse or neglect. There is a degree of unease and uncertainty about how compatible the policy of personalisation (which is essentially a consumer-based, free-market approach to social care) is with the idea of protecting vulnerable adults. In particular, the belief that empowering people will in itself lead to their better protection[2] depends at the very least on more vulnerable people being given adequate support in order to achieve that empowerment. It is not clear that in practice local authorities will be able to achieve this.

KEY ELEMENTS OF PERSONALISATION
The key elements of personalisation emerge from general guidance issued by central government[3] and a range of documents of indeterminate and minimal legal status placed on the internet.[4]

---

1   Her Majesty's Government (2007) *Putting People First: A Shared Vision and Commitment to the Transformation of Adult Social Care.* London: HMG. And: Secretary of State for Health (2005) *Independence, Well-Being and Choice.* Cm 6499. Green Paper. London: TSO.
2   Department of Health (2009) *Safeguarding Adults – Report on the Consultation on the Review of 'No secrets'.* London: DH, para 2.4.
3   LAC(2008)1. Department of Health. *Transforming Social Care.* London: DH. And: LAC(2009)1. Department of Health. *Transforming Social Care.* London: DH.
4   *Personalisation Toolkit.* Available at www.dhcarenetworks.org.uk/Personalisation/Topics, accessed on 18 May 2009.

First, people should be able to determine their own needs by increased use of *self-assessment*. Second, once the level of a person's needs is established, a fixed sum of money will be allocated to the person. This will be achieved by the operation of a *resource allocation system* (RAS); this is a formula for transmuting levels of need into points, and points into a *personal budget*. Third, the person will then be asked (and sometimes helped) to decide how this personal budget should be used to achieve agreed *outcomes*. Fourth, the personal budget can then either be paid as a *direct payment*, or be dealt with as *notional budget* on the person's behalf by a broker or agent.

Fifth, to the extent that people require support with assessment, decisions about services and arranging services, 'support brokerage' should be in place to give people help, advice and advocacy. This might involve local authority staff, independent organisations or individuals, or even family members. Central government has stated that social workers should provide less assessment and more advice and brokerage.

Sixth, in future, the government intends that additional pots of money from other welfare funding sources could be added to the community-care personal budget. The Welfare Reform Act 2009 will make this possible. Regulations yet to be made under it will spell out the detail of how it will all work. Other funding streams might be, for example, access to work grants, the Independent Living Fund, disabled facilities grants, Supporting People moneys (housing support).[5]

LEGAL ISSUES ARISING FROM PERSONALISATION
Personalisation is not yet underpinned by new legislation. So the elements outlined above must by definition fit within existing community care legislation. A number of issues arise.

SELF-ASSESSMENT AND GENERAL OUTCOMES
First, the NHS and Community Care Act, s.47, states that it is for the local authority to assess and decide needs and services. This sits uneasily with the notion of people assessing themselves. The local authority legally cannot give up its overall control of the process. Directions issued some years ago under the 1990 Act do stipulate that the local authority must

---

5   Secretary of State for Work and Pensions (2008) White Paper, Cm 7506. *Raising Expectations and Increasing Support: Reforming Welfare for the Future.* London: TSO, Chapter 3. Also: Office for Disability Issues (2009) *Making Choice and Control a Reality for Disabled People.* London: ODI, p.20.

consult with and seek to reach agreement with the person.[6] However, it is the authority that must have the final word. In addition is the danger that as a result of self-assessment, a local authority might still take the final decision but on the basis of incomplete information. This, too, could be held unlawful, if the local authority could not show it had taken reasonable steps to ensure that an adequate assessment was carried out.[7]

Second, if people's needs are expressed in terms of general outcomes only (e.g. greater involvement in the community), rather than specific services (e.g. attendance at a day centre five times a week), it may be difficult to establish whether a local authority is actually meeting a person's needs. Whereas more detailed care plans provide a legal measure against which a local authority's duty to meet need can be gauged.[8]

RESOURCE ALLOCATION SYSTEMS AND PERSONAL BUDGETS

The allocation of fixed amounts of money relative to need is likely to lead in practice to tight financial capping in order to contain expenditure. As community care rules stand, allocation of insufficient money to meet a person's assessed need is unlawful. Thus, a crude approach to resource allocation may lead to legal problems.

This occurred in a children's case involving a piece of legislation that applies equally to adults, namely, s.2 of the Chronically Sick and Disabled Person Act 1970. Applying a resource-allocation type system to a disabled boy, the local authority placed him in the highest category of need. This equated to a set amount of money and hours of help he could get. As a result he lost half his care, compared with the position before the new system was applied. This was held to be unlawful in light of the duty to meet the boy's needs under the 1970 Act.[9] The judge pointed out that the council could have avoided acting unlawfully if it had built in a degree of flexibility in its allocation system and decision. Department of Health guidance has made the same point in relation to direct payments guidance; resource allocation calculations should be indicative only and not exclude consideration of individual circumstances.[10]

---

6   Department of Health (2004) *Community Care Assessment Directions.* London: DH.
7   *R(B) v Cornwall County Council* [2009] EWHC 491 (Admin).
8   *R v Islington London Borough Council, ex p Rixon* [1997] 1 ELR 477.
9   *R(JL) v Islington London Borough Council* [2009] EWHC 458 (Admin).
10   Department of Health (2009) *Guidance on Direct Payments for Community Care ...* para 113.

PEOPLE'S ELIGIBILITY FOR PERSONAL BUDGETS

Personal budgets will only be available to those deemed eligible under the fair access to care policies of local authorities.[11] The trend over the past decade is that ever fewer people are treated as eligible.[12]

SAFEGUARDING ADULTS

It is beyond the scope of this book to set out in detail the extensive amount of law relevant to safeguarding adults. However, during the 1990s, concern grew about the phenomenon of adult abuse – and a corresponding need for protection and safeguarding. In 2000, the Department of Health published guidance called *No Secrets*. The guidance gave local social services authorities the lead in the development of local policies and practices, involving cooperative working with other local agencies, including the police, housing organisations, NHS bodies, etc.[13] However, no new social services legislation was passed. During 2009, central government in England consulted on whether the guidance should be updated and specific legislation passed,[14] as has occurred in Scotland.[15] In early 2010, it announced that local safeguarding adults boards would be made statutory – and that new *No Secrets* guidance would be issued. In order to understand the legal framework, a twofold approach is required.

First, from the social services point of view, safeguarding issues have to be set in the context of existing community care legislation and related guidance such as that on fair access to care.[16]

Second, in order to understand how other agencies are able to act, an appreciation of other, non-social services legislation is needed – in order to identify possible legal remedies to prevent or to respond to certain types of abuse or neglect. This includes, for example, legislation concerning the barring and monitoring of people who work with vulnerable adults,[17] criminal records certificates,[18] mental capacity legislation,[19] police powers of intervention,[20] and a range of criminal

11 LAC(2008)1. Department of Health *Transforming Social Care*. London: DH, para 19.
12 Commission for Social Care Inspection (2008) *The State of Social Care in England 2006–07*. London: CSCI, p.6.
13 Department of Health (2000) *No Secrets*. London: DH, 2000.
14 Department of Health (2009) *Safeguarding Adults: A Consultation on the Review of 'No Secrets'*. London: DH.
15 *Adult Support and Protection (Scotland) Act 2007*.
16 LAC(2002)13. Department of Health. *Fair Access to Care Services: Guidance on Eligibility Criteria for Adult Social Care*. London: DH.
17 *Safeguarding of Vulnerable Groups Act 2007*.
18 *Police Act 1997*, ss.112–115.
19 *Mental Capacity Act 2005*.
20 E.g. *Police and Criminal Evidence Act 1984*, s.17.

law encompassing, for example, assault and battery, assisted suicide,[21] manslaughter through gross negligence, sexual offences,[22] theft and fraud,[23] etc.

---

21 *Suicide Act 1961.*
22 *Sexual Offences Act 2003.*
23 *Theft Act 1968.*

CHAPTER 10

Asylum and immigration

- Community care: asylum seekers and others subject to immigration control
  - 'Destitution plus' test
  - Low threshold for supporting asylum seekers
  - Care and attention otherwise available
  - Home Office responsibilities
- Asylum seekers with children
- Unaccompanied children
  - Age assessments
- People subject to immigration control other than active asylum seekers
  - Prohibition on helping people
  - Two classes of failed asylum seeker
  - Human rights
  - European Economic Area nationals
- NHS provision and overseas visitors
  - Ordinary residence and the NHS
  - Lawful residence for 12 months
  - Exemption from charges for certain services
  - Exemption from charges: people's status
  - Asylum seekers
  - Immediately necessary, urgent or non-urgent treatment
  - Bilateral health care arrangements
  - Debt recovery

SUMMARY

Since 1996, some local authorities have found themselves heavily involved in providing residential accommodation and related services for asylum seekers and some other people subject to immigration control. The rules about this have been subject to continual change, legal challenge and confusion. This represents an additional and unexpected layer of complexity in the community care system, overlain by significant human rights issues. Asylum seekers and others would have little chance of understanding the rules; local authority practitioners likewise have toiled to work out whether and how to assess people and to provide them with assistance.

Separate rules about 'overseas visitors' apply to the NHS about health care. They, too, have become complex and confusing and given rise to major legal challenge.

COMMUNITY CARE: ASYLUM SEEKERS AND OTHERS SUBJECT TO IMMIGRATION CONTROL

The main pieces of legislation affecting social services provision for asylum seekers and others subject to immigration control are:

(a) the National Assistance Act 1948 and other community care legislation

(b) the Immigration and Asylum Act 1999

(c) the Nationality, Immigration and Asylum Act 2002, and

(d) the Human Rights Act 1998.

'DESTITUTION PLUS' TEST

Under the Immigration and Asylum Act 1999, local authorities are prohibited from assisting asylum seekers with community care, if the need arises solely (a) because the person is destitute, or (b) because of the physical effects, or anticipated physical effects, of destitution. A person is defined as destitute if he or she does not have adequate accommodation or cannot meet other essential living needs.[1] The courts have held that mental illness counts as a physical effect of destitution; but that if there is another likely cause of the mental illness, other than

---

1   *Immigration and Asylum Act 1999*, s.95.

the destitution, then the local authority would not be prohibited from assisting.[2]

The test applies to others, apart from asylum seekers; for example, people lawfully present in the United Kingdom but on condition of not having recourse to public funds. The prohibition from providing services applies to residential accommodation under the National Assistance Act 1948 and some other community care services – but not to s.2 of the Chronically Sick and Disabled Persons Act 1970 (non-residential services for disabled people) or s.117 of the Mental Health Act 1983 (aftercare for detained patients).[3]

LOW THRESHOLD FOR SUPPORTING ASYLUM SEEKERS

For residential accommodation under s.21 of the National Assistance Act 1948, an asylum seeker is eligible for assistance if his or her basic need for care and attention (arising from destitution) is to a material extent made more acute by age, illness, disability or any other circumstances.[4]

This means the normal test of eligibility for community care services ('fair access to care': see Chapter 4) does not apply to asylum seekers. Assistance should be given not just to those asylum seekers who would normally be eligible even without being destitute, but also to those whose needs would not normally qualify. So, asylum seekers have a substantially better chance of qualifying for s.21 accommodation than the local population. For instance, an asylum seeker with a leg abnormality who needed help with bed-making, hoovering and heavy shopping was deemed eligible for s.21 accommodation,[5] as was a woman with spinal cancer who required wheelchair accessible accommodation.[6]

Even so the courts have put in place some limits. The care and attention must involve an element of 'looking after' such as personal care, help with household tasks, help with shopping – but a need for health services doesn't count. Thus, a man with AIDS requiring NHS medication, refrigeration for that medication and NHS appointments – but not needing to be looked after – was not eligible under s.21 of the 1948 Act.[7] This rule was also applied to a person who had undergone

2   *R(PB) v Haringey London Borough Council* [2006] EWHC Admin 2255.
3   *National Assistance Act 1948*, s.21(1A); *Health Services and Public Health Act 1968*, s.45(4A); *NHS Act 2006*, schedule 20, para 6.
4   *R v Wandsworth London Borough Council, ex p O* (2000) 3 CCLR 237, Court of Appeal; *Westminster v NASS (National Asylum Support Service)* [2002] UKHL 38.
5   *R(Mani) v Lambeth London Borough Council* [2003] EWCA Civ 836.
6   *Westminster v NASS (National Asylum Support Service)* [2002] UKHL 38.
7   *R(M) v Slough Borough Council* [2008] UKHL 52.

a cancer operation and who was receiving physiotherapy for neck and back pain but who could cope with activities of daily living[8] – and also to a person who had been an inpatient with tuberculosis, meningitis, syphilis and HIV, but now had no need of help with essential daily living tasks.[9] However, a blind person who needed help to find his way round – and with dressing, laundry, shopping and eating – did need looking after under s.21.[10]

CARE AND ATTENTION OTHERWISE AVAILABLE

The care and attention must be not otherwise available. In one case a local authority argued successfully that a man, lawfully in England but with no recourse to public funds, had care and attention otherwise available – because he could reasonably return to his family in the United States or to his wife with whom he was not currently living.[11]

HOME OFFICE RESPONSIBILITIES

The Home Office has a power to support destitute asylum seekers under s.95 of the Immigration and Asylum Act 1999, unless local authorities are responsible under community care legislation. Likewise under s.4 of the 1999 Act, the Home Office has discretion to provide accommodation for failed asylum seekers who are unable to return to their country of origin. This is known as 'hard cases' support.[12]

ASYLUM SEEKERS WITH CHILDREN

If an adult asylum seeker eligible for social services assistance has a child, then the Home Office is normally responsible for supporting the child.[13] To avoid fragmented practical arrangements, the courts have stated that the local authority should make arrangements for the child on the Home Office's behalf.[14]

---

8   R(Sharef) v Coventry City Council [2009] EWHC 2191 Admin (permission to apply for judicial review).
9   R(N) v Coventry City Council [2008] EWHC 2786 Admin.
10 R(Zarzour) v Hillingdon London Borough Council [2009] EWHC 1398 Admin.
11 R(P) v Camden London Borough Council [2004] EWHC 55.
12 SI 2005/930. The Immigration and Asylum (Provision of Accommodation to Failed Asylum-Seekers) Regulations 2005.
13 Immigration and Asylum Act 1999, s.95.
14 R(O) v Haringey London Borough Council [2004] EWCA Civ 535.

UNACCOMPANIED CHILDREN

An unaccompanied child, who is an asylum seeker or otherwise subject to immigration control, is the potential responsibility of the local authority under the Children Act 1989. Such support is prohibited neither in s.122 of the Immigration and Asylum Act 1999 nor in schedule 3 of the Nationality, Immigration and Asylum Act 2002 (see below).

There is a legal presumption that accommodation provided for unaccompanied asylum seeking children will be under s.20 of the 1989 Act rather than s.17.[15] Section 20 triggers the so-called 'leaving care' rules, involving support from the local authority when the child leaves care.[16]

AGE ASSESSMENTS

Assessing whether somebody is a child or adult is legally significant as to what help, if any, he or she is entitled to. Local authorities should not avoid making such an assessment where it is clearly called for.[17] They should not unquestioningly follow the Home Office's view but come to their own conclusions, should explain the purpose of the interview to the person, and give him or her opportunity to address the issues.[18] All relevant factors should be taken into account[19] including relevant medical opinion,[20] and common sense analysis be applied to evidence such as dental reports.[21] However, a local authority need not always seek expert medical advice, and the weight to be attached to such advice will vary; a local authority may rely on the assessment of a suitably experienced and trained social worker.[22] Ultimately a child's age is an objective fact that has to be established, and is not just down to the subjective view of a local authority. For that reason, age is a legal question that can be decided by the courts.[23]

---

15 R(Berhe) Hillingdon London Borough Council [2003] EWHC Admin 2075; R(G) v Southwark London Borough Council [2009] UKHL 26.

16 Children Act 1989, ss.23–24.

17 R(Liverpool City Council) v Hillingdon London Borough Council [2009] EWCA Civ 43.

18 R(B) v Merton London Borough Council [2003] EWHC Admin 1689.

19 R(T) v Enfield London Borough Council [2004] EWHC Admin 2297.

20 R(C) v Merton LBC [2005] EWHC Admin 1753.

21 R(A) v Liverpool City Council [2007] EWHC 1477 Admin.

22 A v Croydon London Borough Council [2009] EWHC 939 Admin.

23 R(A) v Croydon London Borough Council [2009] UKSC 8.

PEOPLE SUBJECT TO IMMIGRATION CONTROL OTHER THAN ACTIVE ASYLUM SEEKERS

For some people subject to immigration control, social services are barred from providing support or assistance for adults under both community care legislation (except s.117 of the Mental Health Act 1983) and the Children Act 1989. This prohibition comes under the Nationality, Immigration and Asylum Act 2002. However, assistance is not prohibited for children – or if failure to assist would be a breach of human rights or of a European Community treaty.

PROHIBITION ON HELPING PEOPLE

The prohibition in the 2002 Act applies to (a) people who have refugee status abroad, (b) some people who are members of a European Economic Area state other than the United Kingdom, (c) failed asylum seekers who are not cooperating with removal directions, (d) any other person, not an asylum seeker, who is in breach of the immigration laws.

The prohibitions placed on a local authority's ability to provide support for an adult subject to immigration control (other than an asylum seeker) does contain an exception – if he or she is accompanied by a dependent child.[24]

TWO CLASSES OF FAILED ASYLUM SEEKER

There are legally two classes of failed asylum seeker. First, a failed asylum seeker who claimed asylum at point of entry to the United Kingdom, and who has not yet failed to cooperate with removal directions, continues to be eligible for social services support under the 2002 Act rules.

Second, a failed asylum seeker who did not claim asylum on entry, but only later and 'in-country', is deemed to be in breach of immigration law – and so is straightaway denied social services support on failure of the claim (unless human rights would be breached).[25]

Except in case of manifest inadequacy, a further claim for asylum on human rights grounds means that a local authority will have to provide support for a failed asylum seeker pending the Home Office's decision.[26]

---

24 SI 2002/3078. *Withholding and Withdrawal of Support (Travel Assistance and Temporary Accommodation) Regulations 2002*.

25 *R(AW) v Croydon London Borough Council* [2007] EWCA Civ 266, Court of Appeal.

26 *R(AW) v Croydon London Borough Council* [2007] EWCA Civ 266, Court of Appeal. Also: *R(Binomugisha) v Southwark London Borough Council* [2006] EWHC Admin 2254.

A failed asylum seeker with a dependent child remains eligible for Home Office support.[27]

HUMAN RIGHTS

The prohibitions placed on local social services authorities in schedule 3 of the 2002 Act do not apply if a person's human rights (or rights under European Community law) would otherwise be breached; likewise the prohibitions placed on Home Office assistance under s.55 of the Act. Leaving asylum seekers to sleep in the street, experience serious hunger and lack basic hygiene requirements may indicate inhuman or degrading treatment under article 3 of the European Convention on Human Rights.[28]

In relation to deportation, a major case involved a woman with AIDS who had been seriously ill-treated in Uganda by the Lord's Resistance Army, and ill-treated and raped by the National Resistance Movement (part of the Ugandan security forces). She was a failed asylum seeker. The European Court of Human Rights held that the fact that life expectancy would be reduced significantly, because the standard of treatment in another country would be considerably lower, did not necessarily mean that article 3 would be breached by removal. Exceptionally, it might do so, but not in this particular case.[29]

Of importance, therefore, in ascertaining a local authority's potential obligations – to avoid a breach of human rights – is the question of whether the person is able to return to his or her own country, freely and without impediment,[30] perhaps with assistance (e.g. an air ticket) from the local authority. In such cases, the local authority in effect asks whether there would be a human rights breach in the destination country, rather than such a breach if the person were to remain on the streets in the United Kingdom.[31] This in turn means that if a local authority already has clear information (a) about a person's immigration status (e.g. a failed asylum seeker), and (b) about there being nothing to stop him or her returning to country of origin, then it might not have to carry out a community care assessment or reassessment.[32]

---

27 *Immigration and Asylum Act 1999*, s.94.
28 *R v Secretary of State for the Home Department, ex p Adam, Limbuela, Tesema* [2005] UKHL 66, House of Lords.
29 *N v United Kingdom* (2008), European Court of Human Rights (Application 26565/05, 27 May 2008).
30 *R(K) v Lambeth London Borough Council* [2003] EWCA Civ 1150.
31 *R(N) v Coventry City Council* [2008] EWHC 2786 Admin.
32 *R(Sharef) v Coventry City Council* [2009] EWHC 2191 Admin.

EUROPEAN ECONOMIC AREA NATIONALS

People from the European Economic Area are excluded from support under schedule 3 of the 2002 Act, unless this would breach a European Community treaty.[33] Generally speaking, European Economic Area nationals – who have worked or work in the United Kingdom, their families, self-employed and former self-employed people and students – are eligible for assistance from social services.[34] The rules are modified for the eight so-called accession countries (Poland, Lithuania, Estonia, Latvia, Slovenia, Slovakia, Hungary and the Czech Republic).

NHS PROVISION AND OVERSEAS VISITORS

NHS trusts have a duty to charge overseas visitors for hospital services. However, certain services are exempt from this rule, as are certain categories of people according to their status. These rules apply to hospital secondary care services only and not to primary health care services. The legal rules are contained in regulations made under s.175 of the NHS Act 2006.[35] In addition, the Department of Health has published guidance.[36]

ORDINARY RESIDENCE AND THE NHS

The NHS has a duty to establish whether people are ordinarily resident in the United Kingdom, to assess liability for charges and to charge those liable to pay.[37] This is a key question because if people are ordinarily resident, then they are entitled to NHS services as normal and are not categorised as overseas visitors.

Ordinary residence is legally about a person being in a 'particular place or country which he has adopted voluntarily and for settled purposes as part of the regular order of his life for the time being, whether of long or short duration'.[38] The guidance suggests that a person should be resident for at least six months, but this is not a hard and fast rule and is not a legal minimum.[39]

---

33 And in particular: SI 2006/1003. *Immigration (European Economic Area) Regulations 2006.*
34 Department of Health (2003) *Section 54 of the Nationality, Immigration and Asylum Act 2002 and Community Care and other Social Services for Adults from the European Economic Area Living in the UK.* London: DH.
35 SI 1989/306. *National Health Service (Charges to Overseas Visitors) Regulations 1989.*
36 Department of Health (2007) *Implementing the Overseas Visitors Hospital Charging Regulations: Guidance for NHS Trust Hospitals in England.* London: DH.
37 SI 1989/306. *National Health Service (Charges to Overseas Visitors) Regulations 1989,* r.2.
38 *R v Barnet London Borough Council, ex p Shah* (1983) 2 AC 309, House of Lords.
39 Department of Health (2007) *Implementing the Overseas Visitors ... p.51.*

LAWFUL RESIDENCE FOR 12 MONTHS

Apart from the question of ordinary residence, there is anyway an exemption from charges for overseas visitors who have been resident lawfully in the United Kingdom for at least 12 months.[40]

EXEMPTION FROM CHARGES FOR CERTAIN SERVICES

Some services must be provided free to everyone, regardless of their status, including treatment at an accident and emergency or casualty department or a walk-in centre providing the same services. Treatment is also free for: family planning services, certain diseases to protect the wider public health (a list of exempt diseases is included in the regulations), initial diagnostic test and associated counselling (but not treatment) for HIV/AIDS, and people detained or received into guardianship under the Mental Health Act 1983.[41]

Health services – not provided by a hospital, by staff employed to work at a hospital, or under the direction of a hospital – are also exempt.[42]

EXEMPTION FROM CHARGES: PEOPLE'S STATUS

There is a long list of exemptions based on a person's status. These include students pursuing a course of study longer than six months (or less than six months but substantially funded by the United Kingdom government), refugees, a number of exceptions related to employment arrangements, United Kingdom pensioners who reside in the United Kingdom for at least six months each year and in another member State for less than six months a year and who are not registered as resident of another member State – and British nationals or others with a right of abode who return to the United Kingdom to resume permanent residence. Victims, or suspected victims, of human trafficking are also exempt.[43]

ASYLUM SEEKERS

Department of Health guidance states that refugees and asylum seekers are exempt from charges if they have made a formal application to the

---

40 SI 1989/306. *National Health Service (Charges to Overseas Visitors) Regulations 1989*, rr.2,4.
41 SI 1989/306. *National Health Service (Charges to Overseas Visitors) Regulations 1989*, rr.2, 3.
42 Department of Health (2007) *Implementing the Overseas Visitors ...* para 6.7.
43 SI 1989/306. *National Health Service (Charges to Overseas Visitors) Regulations 1989*. And: Department of Health (2007) *Implementing the Overseas Visitors ...* paras 25–30.

Home Office, which has not yet been decided. Exemption only lasts until that decision. If an application for asylum fails, existing treatment being given must be completed. Any new course of treatment will be charged for. Even if failed asylum seekers have completed 12 months residence they will not be exempt.[44]

IMMEDIATELY NECESSARY, URGENT OR NON-URGENT TREATMENT
Guidance tells NHS trusts when to provide necessary, urgent or non-urgent treatment.[45] If provided, any such treatment remains chargeable unless it falls into an exempt category (as discussed above).

In 2009, the courts held that this guidance was unclear.[46] Ahead of redrafting the guidance, the Department of Health issued interim guidance. This stated that immediately necessary treatment, including all maternity treatment, should never be withheld for any reason. But it should be limited to what is necessary to enable people to return to their own country, although NHS trusts should take account of the likelihood of the person returning home.

Urgent treatment is not immediately necessary, but cannot wait until the person can reasonably be expected to return home. Any intervening period ahead of treatment should be used to secure payment, but if this is not forthcoming, treatment should not be withheld. Whenever possible, deposits should be sought.

Non-urgent treatment is routine, elective treatment, which could wait until the patient returns home. If the patient does not return home, and the treatment remains non-urgent, then it should not be given until payment has been received.[47]

BILATERAL HEALTH CARE ARRANGEMENTS
Bilateral health care arrangements exist between member states of the European Economic Area (EEA) and Switzerland. Residents of these countries are entitled to treatment if they have a form E112 – or if the treatment is immediately necessary. There are also bilateral agreements

44 Department of Health (2007) *Implementing the Overseas Visitors* ... para 6.24. And see: *R(YA) v Secretary of State for Health* [2009] EWCA Civ 225.
45 Department of Health (2007) *Implementing the Overseas Visitors* ...
46 *R(YA) v Secretary of State for Health* [2009] EWCA Civ 225.
47 Department of Health (2009) *Advice for Overseas Visitors Managers on 1a) Failed Asylum Seekers and Ordinary/Lawful Residence 1b) When to Provide Treatment for Those Who are Chargeable; 2) Victims of Human Trafficking.* London: DH.

between the United Kingdom and some other countries.[48] Special rules apply to the eight recent accession countries to the European Union.[49]

DEBT RECOVERY

The regulations place a duty on NHS trusts to make charges, if overseas visitors are not exempt.[50] Guidance states that bad debt cannot simply be waived. It recommends the NHS use specialist debt-recovery agencies. Debt that proves irrecoverable should be written off and properly recorded. Invoices should still be raised even if it is believed the person cannot pay. The NHS can write-off debt if all reasonable steps for recovery have been taken, or the patient has died.[51]

48 Department of Health (2007) *Implementing the Overseas Visitors* ... p.29.
49 Department of Health (2007) *National Health Service (Charges to Overseas) Regulations 1989. Notification of Changes: Amended 30 April 2007.* London: DH.
50 SI 1989/306. *National Health Service (Charges to Overseas Visitors) Regulations 198*, r.2.
51 Department of Health (2007) *Implementing the Overseas Visitors* ... p.44.

CHAPTER 11

Ordinary residence

- Social services: ordinary residence
  - Meaning of 'ordinarily resident'
  - Deeming provisions
  - Moving from residential accommodation into the community
  - Children leaving care
  - Ordinary residence of people in hospital, nursing homes, prison and similar establishments
  - Ordinary residence disputes affecting services
- NHS responsible commissioner
  - Registration with general practitioner
  - Prisons
  - Mental Health Act 1983
  - NHS continuing health care
  - Funded nursing care

SUMMARY

A person's residence can affect the obligations of both local social services authorities and the NHS. This is because some duties are conditional on a person being resident within the area of a local authority or NHS primary care trust.

The resource implications can be considerable. This is why local authorities sometimes engage in frequent and sometimes lengthy disputes. And, as the NHS becomes more fragmented, with NHS providers urged to compete with each other, disputes about residence and the 'responsible commissioner' are seemingly more prevalent. Department of Health guidance states that disputes should in any event not be allowed to cause detriment to the service user.

SOCIAL SERVICES: ORDINARY RESIDENCE

Some local authority obligations to provide community care services (both residential and non-residential) depend on whether a person is 'ordinarily resident' in the authority's area. For example, a duty towards an 'ordinary resident' to arrange a care home placement is only a power in the case of a non-resident of the area, under s.21 of the National Assistance Act 1948.

The courts have noted that a person without settled residence is less well protected legally;[1] however, guidance advises that the local authority where he or she presents him- or herself should normally accept responsibility.[2] A power towards somebody of no settled residence is anyway converted to a duty in cases of urgency; and physical presence in the area of a local authority is then enough to trigger this duty.[3] See Chapter 5.

Under s.29 of the 1948 Act, a duty to provide certain non-residential services for disabled people is changed to a power only in the case of those not ordinarily resident. And the strong duty under s.2 of the Chronically Sick and Disabled Persons Act 1970 extends to ordinary residents only.

MEANING OF 'ORDINARILY RESIDENT'

Ordinary residence is defined legally as a person's 'abode in a particular place or country which he has adopted voluntarily and for settled purposes as part of the regular order of his life for the time being, whether of short or long duration'.[4]

DEEMING PROVISIONS

If a person is placed in residential accommodation (usually a care home), he or she is deemed legally to be ordinarily resident in the area in which he or she was ordinarily resident immediately before the placement.[5]

This means that if a person is placed in a care home by one local authority in the area of another local authority, then it is the former that retains responsibility. However, if the person privately moves to another local authority area, he or she may become ordinarily resident there. If he or she then goes into a care home and needs social services help, it will fall to that second local authority.[6]

---

1   R(Greenwich) v Secretary of State for Health [2006] EWHC Admin 2576.
2   LAC(93)7. Department of Health. *Ordinary Residence.* London: DH, para 16.
3   R(S) v Lewisham LBC, Lambeth LBC, Hackney LBC [2008] EWHC 1290 Admin.
4   R v Barnet London Borough Council, ex p Shah (1983) 2 AC 309, House of Lords.
5   *National Assistance Act 1948*, s.24.
6   LAC(93)7. Department of Health. *Ordinary Residence.* London: DH, paras 7, 10.

Similarly if people move privately to a care home in the second local authority (even if assisted to do so by the first local authority), their funds then run down and they then need social services assistance, it will be the responsibility of the second authority. Unsurprisingly, this rule can lead to allegations, justified or not, by the second authority against the first of 'dumping' people.[7]

MOVING FROM RESIDENTIAL ACCOMMODATION INTO THE COMMUNITY

If a person, placed by the first local authority in a care home in the area of a second authority, leaves the care home voluntarily and lives in the community in the area of second authority, the latter is normally responsible for non-residential community care services now needed, typically under the Chronically Sick and Disabled Persons Act 1970.

If the person lacks the capacity to decide to move out of a care home into the community, there are two key points. First, it must be confirmed that the person really did lack this capacity. Second, assuming actual lack of capacity, nonetheless the person should be taken to have capacity and residence decided on the facts of the case, in terms of his or her actual connections and dependency.[8] The same question may also arise when a care home deregisters and the ex-residents suddenly become tenants in a supported living environment.[9]

The stakes may be very high and lead to desperate measures. In one case, a local authority unsuccessfully argued that a woman with severe mental health problems was an NHS responsibility. The care package came to an annual cost of £675,000. Undaunted, the local authority then succeeded in a second legal case, this time against another local authority. It had placed the woman in a community setting in the area of the second authority – which now had to pick up the responsibility.[10]

CHILDREN LEAVING CARE

Ordinary residence questions arise under the National Assistance Act 1948 when a local authority has previously taken responsibility under the Children Act 1989 and placed the child in another local authority area – and the child then turns 18 years old. To establish ordinary

7   R(Greenwich) v Secretary of State for Health [2006] EWHC Admin 2576.
8   Secretary of State for Health 2005, ordinary residence determination no.5. Following the approach in: R v Waltham Forest London Borough Council, ex p Vale [1985] TLR, 25 February 1985.
9   Secretary of State for Health 2006, ordinary residence determination no.3.
10 St. Helens Borough Council v Manchester Primary Care Trust [2008] EWCA 931 Civ; R(Manchester City Council) v St. Helens Borough Council [2009] EWCA 1348 Civ.

residence under the 1989 Act, the period in which a child lives in accommodation arranged by the local authority should be disregarded. So, up to a person's 18th birthday the child remains ordinarily resident in the original area.[11] Then, however, ordinary residence has instead to be determined under the 1948 Act.

In deciding disputes between local authorities, the Secretary of State has held that ordinary residence under the Children Act is an important, but not decisive, factor in deciding ordinary residence under the 1948 Act.[12] Similarly, guidance states that local authorities could 'reasonably have regard' to the definition in the 1989 Act, for the purposes of the 1948 Act.[13]

If the person has capacity, the normal ordinary residence test applies.[14] For instance, where a person had retained contact with his mother in the first local authority but had put down roots in a second authority, had friends there, participated in outside activities, had a part-time job and indicated he wished to remain in that second authority, then he was ordinarily resident in that second area.[15]

If the person lacks capacity, the approach to be taken is to assume the person has capacity and determine where his or her main connections and base are.[16] So, a person might be totally dependent on his or her parents still, and so remain ordinarily resident at their address, even though he or she has been in care for many years in another local authority.[17] Alternatively, ordinary residence might be in the council area in which the care placement has been made – if the person has lost contact with his parents for years.[18]

ORDINARY RESIDENCE OF PEOPLE IN HOSPITAL, NURSING HOMES, PRISON AND SIMILAR ESTABLISHMENTS

An NHS patient is deemed to be ordinarily resident, for local authority purposes, in the area (if any) he or she was living in immediately before entering an NHS hospital.[19] This part of the legislation is due to change, and will in future refer to NHS accommodation (not just hospitals)

---

11 *Children Act 1989*, s.105(6).
12 Secretary of State 2006, ordinary residence determination no.4.
13 LAC(93)7. Department of Health. *Ordinary Residence.* London: DH, para 21.
14 *R v Barnet London Borough Council, ex p Shah* (1983) 2 AC 309, House of Lords.
15 Secretary of State for Health 2007, ordinary residence determination no.3.
16 *R v Waltham Forest London Borough Council, ex p Vale* [1985] TLR, 25 February 1985.
17 Secretary of State 2005, ordinary residence determination no.3.
18 Secretary of State 2005, ordinary residence determination no.1.
19 *National Assistance Act 1948*, s.24.

generally and also in particular to NHS provision of accommodation under s.117 of the Mental Health Act 1983.[20]

Guidance suggests local authorities could apply this approach to people in comparable situations, such as prisons, resettlement units and other such establishments. These people might be without a permanent place to live and might require social services involvement at the time of their discharge.[21] Determining residence can become complicated when hospital or hospital-like stays – either for a lengthy time or involving several establishments – are in issue.[22]

ORDINARY RESIDENCE DISPUTES AFFECTING SERVICES

When disputes about ordinary residence arise between local authorities, guidance states that delay in assessment and service provision should not occur.[23] A failure to follow this guidance will attract judicial censure[24] or findings of maladministration by the local ombudsman.[25] Disputes about ordinary residence should ultimately be determined by the Secretary of State.[26] This procedure covers disputes about residential accommodation and also non-residential services under s.29 of the 1948 Act. The legislation is due to change to clarify that this dispute procedure applies also to s.2 of the Chronically Sick and Disabled Persons Act 1970.[27]

NHS RESPONSIBLE COMMISSIONER

The legal framework regarding NHS commissioning responsibilities is set out in regulations affecting primary care trusts (PCTs),[28] which are responsible for commissioning local health services. Guidance issued by the Department of Health includes a number of key points set out below. It emphasises that treatment should not be delayed or refused because of uncertainty about where somebody is resident.[29]

---

20 Amendment in: s.148 of the *Health and Social Care Act 2008*.
21 LAC(93)7. Department of Health. *Ordinary Residence*. London: DH, para 14.
22 Secretary of State for Health 2005, ordinary residence determination no.7; Secretary of State for Health 2007, ordinary residence determination no.1.
23 LAC(93)7. Department of Health. *Ordinary Residence*. London: DH, Summary, para 3.
24 *R v Hackney London Borough Council, ex p J* (1999) unreported.
25 *Redbridge London Borough Council 1998* (95/C/1472, 95/C/2543).
26 *National Assistance Act 1948*, s.32.
27 Amendment in *Health and Social Care Act 2008*, s.148.
28 SI 2002/2375. *NHS (Functions of Strategic Health Authorities and Primary Care Trusts and Administration Arrangements) (England) Regulations 2002.*
29 Department of Health (2007) *Who pays? Establishing the Responsible Commissioner.* London: DH, para 2.

REGISTRATION WITH GENERAL PRACTITIONER

A PCT is responsible for commissioning services for people registered with a general practitioner (GP) associated with the PCT. It is also responsible for other people usually resident in the area or for non-United Kingdom residents present in the area but not registered with a GP.

In summary, the responsible PCT is identified by the GP with whom a patient is registered or, where not applicable, by the person's usual residence. If a person has no fixed abode, then the address the person gives as their 'usual residence' should determine responsibility; for example, this may be a hostel. If no address of usual residence can be established, then the area in which the person is present establishes responsibility.[30]

If a person moves residence during a course of treatment, the same basic test applies as above. The guidance suggests the original PCT may wish to continue to provide the treatment on behalf of the new PCT for a certain length of time.[31]

PRISONS

The PCT within whose area a prison is located is responsible for commissioning services for the prisoners.[32]

MENTAL HEALTH ACT 1983

For people detained for treatment under the Mental Health Act 1983, the basic test applies. If GP registration or residential address cannot be established, the responsible PCT is determined by the location of the mental health unit.[33] A separate rule governs responsibility for aftercare under s.117 of the Mental Health Act 1983; the responsible PCT is where the person was resident before he or she was detained; if such previous residence is not ascertainable, then responsibility for s.117 services falls on the PCT for the area to which the person is discharged.[34]

30 Department of Health (2007) *Who pays? Establishing the Responsible Commissioner* ... paras 17–18.
31 Department of Health (2007) *Who pays? Establishing the Responsible Commissioner* ... para 19.
32 Department of Health (2007) *Who pays? Establishing the Responsible Commissioner* ... paras 84–85.
33 Department of Health (2007) *Who pays? Establishing the Responsible Commissioner* ... para 64.
34 *R v Mental Health Review Tribunal, Torfaen County Borough Council and Gwent Health Authority, ex p Hall* (1999) 2 CCLR 361, Administrative Division.

NHS CONTINUING HEALTH CARE

In the case of NHS continuing health care (see Chapter 14), the original, placing PCT remains responsible for a placement in residential accommodation (care home or independent hospital), even if the placement is in another area. If continuing health care is provided in a person's own home, then responsibility is ascertained under the usual rules; likewise if the person is transferred to an NHS hospital for inpatient care.[35]

FUNDED NURSING CARE

If a person is placed in a nursing home outside the original PCT, it is the receiving PCT that becomes responsible for the funded nursing care element of the care home fee – albeit after being informed by the original PCT.[36]

---

35 Department of Health (2007) *Who pays? Establishing the Responsible Commissioner* ... Annex C.
36 Department of Health (2007) *Who pays? Establishing the Responsible Commissioner* ... Annex C.

CHAPTER 12

Home adaptations

- Disabled facilities grants: Housing Grants, Construction and Regeneration Act 1996
  - Disabled occupant
  - Purposes for which a grant must be awarded
  - Residence and housing tenure
  - Works must be necessary and appropriate
  - Works must be reasonable and practicable
  - Giving reasons and time limits
  - Amount of grant
  - Discretionary assistance
- Social services responsibilities for adaptations

SUMMARY

Department of Health guidance refers to the importance of home adaptations to enable people to remain in their own homes.[1] However, home adaptations rely, legally and practically, on a high degree of cooperation between local social services authorities and local housing authorities (who provide assistance in the form of 'disabled facilities grants').

The system of adaptations has long been beset by funding problems in relation to demand, and consequently by long waiting times. Local housing authorities in some areas attempt to dilute the duty to approve disabled facilities grants by deploying a range of restrictive and legally suspect policies. Practice in local social services authorities seems to vary considerably, some providing substantial assistance for major adaptations under s.2 of 1970 Act, others being most reluctant to do so.

---

1 Department of Health (1990) *Community Care in the Next Decade and Beyond: Policy Guidance.* London: DH, para 3.24.

The Disability Discrimination Act adds some additional duties, on landlords in general, including an obligation not to refuse permission for adaptations unreasonably, and to make reasonable adjustments for disabled tenants by way of minor adaptations and equipment. It is beyond the scope of this book to cover these provisions.

DISABLED FACILITIES GRANTS: HOUSING GRANTS, CONSTRUCTION AND REGENERATION ACT 1996

Housing authorities have a strong and enforceable duty, if certain conditions are met, to approve applications for disabled facilities grants for the carrying out of home adaptations. The conditions are that (a) the adaptation in question falls into one of the purposes in the Act that attract mandatory grant, (b) if so, that it is necessary and appropriate, (c) if so, that it is also reasonable and practicable.[2] The three questions should be asked and answered logically and separately.[3]

DISABLED OCCUPANT

The person to whom the application relates must be disabled, insofar as (a) his or her sight, hearing or speech is substantially impaired, (b) he or she has a mental disorder or impairment of any kind, or (c) he or she is substantially physically disabled by illness, injury, impairment since birth or otherwise.[4]

PURPOSES FOR WHICH A GRANT MUST BE AWARDED

The 1996 Act lists a number of purposes that will in principle attract mandatory grant. These are to facilitate access by the disabled occupant:

(a) to and from the dwelling

(b) to a room used as the *principal family room*

(c) to, or providing for the disabled occupant, a room used or usable for *sleeping*

(d) to, or providing for the disabled occupant, a room in which there is a *lavatory* – or facilitating its use by the disabled occupant

---

2 *Housing Grants, Construction and Regeneration Act 1996*, ss.23–24.

3 *R(B) v Calderdale Metropolitan Borough Council* [2004] EWCA Civ 134, Court of Appeal.

4 *Housing Grants, Construction and Regeneration Act 1996*, s.100.

(e) to, or providing for the disabled occupant, a room in which there is a *bath* or a *shower* (or both) – or facilitating its use by the disabled occupant

(f) to, or providing for the disabled occupant, a room in which there is a *wash-hand basin* – or facilitating its use by the disabled occupant.

Other purposes are:

(g) making the dwelling or building *safe* for the disabled occupant and other persons residing with him or her

(h) facilitating the *preparation and cooking of food* by the disabled occupant

(i) improving any *heating system* in the dwelling to meet the needs of the disabled occupant or – if there is no existing heating system or an existing system is unsuitable for use by the disabled occupant – providing a heating system suitable to meet his or her needs

(j) facilitating the use by the disabled occupant of a source of *power, light or heat* by altering the position of one or more means of access to, or control of, that source – or by providing additional means of control

(k) facilitating access and movement by the disabled occupant around the dwelling in order to *enable him or her to care for a person* who normally resides in the dwelling and needs such care.[5]

Gardens fall legally within mandatory grant in terms both of 'making access to a garden safe for a disabled occupant', and also of 'facilitating access to and from a garden by a disabled occupant'.[6] 'Dwelling' is defined as a building or part of a building occupied or intended to be occupied as a separate dwelling, together with any yard, garden, outhouses and appurtenances belonging to it or usually enjoyed with it.[7]

---

5   *Housing Grants, Construction and Regeneration Act 1996*, s.23.
6   SI 2008/1189. *Disabled Facilities Grants (Maximum Amounts and Additional Purposes) (England) Order 2006.*
7   *Housing Grants, Construction and Regeneration Act 1996*, s.101.

RESIDENCE AND HOUSING TENURE

The residence qualification for DFGs under housing legislation applies to dwelling rather than area of residence (in contrast to social services residence rules: see Chapter 11). The dwelling must be the person's only or main residence, either as owner or occupier of a houseboat or caravan.[8]

Private-sector owner occupiers can apply for disabled facilities grants, as can tenants in different tenures, private, council and housing association or registered social-landlord housing. Landlords can also themselves apply. Significant numbers of local authorities have for many years obstructed applications by council, and sometimes housing association, tenants. Guidance from central government points out that such obstruction is unlawful. It states that councils can offer adaptations to their own tenants other than through DFG, but that the adaptations should be carried out on terms as advantageous as if a DFG had been awarded.[9]

WORKS MUST BE NECESSARY AND APPROPRIATE

The works must be necessary and appropriate. This is a decision for the housing authority to take, but if the housing authority is not itself also a social services authority, then it is under an obligation to consult the latter about this issue.[10] The courts have stated that the decision about whether works are necessary and appropriate is 'directed to a consideration of a technical question'. Local housing authorities are therefore not entitled to take resources into account.[11]

In the light of this judicial decision, both social services and housing authorities must guard against applying the rules for one set of legislation to another. Guidance points out that a person might be eligible for DFG assistance but not for social services assistance.[12] Accordingly, the local ombudsman has found maladministration when a local authority dealt with applications for adaptations by collapsing into one procedure its decision under the HGCRA 1996 and Chronically Sick and Disabled Persons Act 1970.[13]

---

8   *Housing Grants, Construction and Regeneration Act 1996*, ss.21, 22A.
9   Office of the Deputy Prime Minister (2006) *Delivering Housing Adaptations for Disabled People: A Good Practice Guide*. London: ODPM, paras 3.26, 3.21.
10 *Housing Grants, Construction and Regeneration Act 1996*, s.24.
11 *R v Birmingham City Council, ex p Taj Mohammed* [1998] 1 CCLR 441.
12 Office of the Deputy Prime Minister (2006) *Delivering Housing* ... paras 4.7.
13 *Neath Port Talbot County Borough Council 1999* (99/0149/N/142).

WORKS MUST BE REASONABLE AND PRACTICABLE

In addition to deciding whether a proposed adaptation is necessary and appropriate, housing authorities must also decide whether it is reasonable and practicable in relation to the age and condition of the dwelling. Central government guidance gives examples of issues that relate to this condition.[14] The courts have indicated that resources can legitimately inform the decision; for example, it might not be 'sensible use of resources to make a DFG to improve an old dilapidated building, or a dwelling which was not fit for human habitation'.[15]

GIVING REASONS AND TIME LIMITS

Applications for DFGs must be determined within six months from the date of application and reasons given for a refusal. If approved, payment must then be made no longer than 12 months from the original date of application.[16] Guidance states that the 12-month limit should be used sparingly, especially where hardship or suffering would be caused.[17]

In practice, delay is common in many local authorities. If the local authority deliberately stops or prevents people finalising their applications, so that the time limit of six months (for approval) does not start running, this may be unlawful[18] and maladministration in the eyes of the local ombudsman.[19]

AMOUNT OF GRANT

If all the relevant conditions are met, housing authorities are obliged to approve applications for DFGs up to a certain maximum, currently £30,000.[20] Housing authorities have discretion, but no obligation, to exceed this maximum amount of grant by exercising their general discretion (see immediately below).

Once an application has been approved, the applicant will be subject to a test of resources in order to determine his or her contribution to the cost of the works. The test is similar to that applied to housing benefit applications. It does not take account of outgoings. In the case of an adult, only that adult's resources, and those of his or her partner, will

14 Office of the Deputy Prime Minister (2006) *Delivering Housing* ... Annex B, para 37.
15 *R v Birmingham City Council, ex p Taj Mohammed* [1998] 1 CCLR 441.
16 *Housing Grants, Construction and Regeneration Act 1996*, ss.34–36.
17 Office of the Deputy Prime Minister (2006) *Delivering Housing* ... Annex B, para 54.
18 *Qazi v Waltham Forest London Borough Council* (1999) unreported (QBD).
19 *Cardiff City Council 2004* (2003/0671/CF/490).
20 SI 2008/1189. *Disabled Facilities Grants (Maximum Amounts and Additional Purposes) (England) Order 2006.*

be taken into account.[21] In the case of children, the test of resources has been abolished (prior to this abolition, the parents' resources were taken into account).

DISCRETIONARY ASSISTANCE

Under the Regulatory Reform (Housing Assistance) (England and Wales) Order 2002, housing authorities have a wide discretion to assist with housing in their locality.[22]

The assistance can include acquiring living accommodation but also adapting or improving it. The assistance may be provided in any form; it may be unconditional or subject to conditions, including repayment of, or contribution to, the assistance. The housing authority could take security, including a charge over the property. The Order allows local authorities to assist disabled and elderly people in a range of ways including 'topping up' disabled facilities grants beyond the £30,000 maximum, providing help that does not come within the ambit of disabled facilities grants, relocation grants, etc.

A housing authority must, under the Order, have a local, published policy, explaining what assistance it provides. Guidance points out that in order to avoid fettering their discretion, authorities should have a mechanism to consider individual requests, even if they fall outside the scope of the local policy.[23] The local government ombudsman has on a number of occasions expected local authorities to give serious consideration to using such discretion, over and above their duty to award DFGs. The ombudsman has also referred in this respect to the disability equality duty that local authorities have under s.49A of the Disability Discrimination Act 1995 (see Chapter 15).[24] Additional guidance states that local authorities should make 'appropriate provision' to use their discretionary spending powers.[25]

SOCIAL SERVICES RESPONSIBILITIES FOR ADAPTATIONS

Local authorities clearly have responsibilities for adaptations under s.2 of the Chronically Sick and Disabled Persons Act 1970. This states that,

---

21 SI 1996/2890. *Housing Renewal Grants Regulations 1996.*
22 SI 2002/1860. *Regulatory Reform (Housing Assistance) (England and Wales) Order 2002.*
23 ODPM 5/2003. Office of the Deputy Prime Minister. *Housing Renewal.* London: ODPM. London: ODPM, para 4.5.
24 *Kirklees Metropolitan Borough Council 2008* (07/C/05809); *Walsall Metropolitan Borough Council 2008* (07/B/07346).
25 Office of the Deputy Prime Minister (2006) *Delivering Housing …* para 1.9.

once the local social services authority has accepted that it is necessary for it to meet the need, then it must make arrangements for 'provision of assistance for the person in arranging for the carrying out of any works of adaptation in his or her home'. Typically, social services might be asked to 'top up' any shortfall in DFG funding; or, less frequently, even to fund a major adaptation that does fall within the definition of a DFG.

However, the wording of s.2 of the 1970 Act is not straightforward. On the one hand, government guidance takes it to mean that social services might incur significant responsibilities for assisting with major adaptations under s.2.[26] On the other, the Court of Appeal has doubted, though did not state definitively, whether substantial responsibilities for adaptations could arise in respect of adults (it accepted that they could arise for children).[27] The extent of the duty under s.2 is not wholly clear. This explains why practice is so variable. Some local social services authorities regularly top up DFGs and, even occasionally, wholly fund major adaptations; while other local authorities seem to take pride in never doing so.

26 Office of the Deputy Prime Minister (2006) *Delivering Housing* ... para 2.8.

27 *R(Spink) v Wandsworth LBC* [2005] EWCA Civ 302, Court of Appeal.

CHAPTER 13

The National Health Service

- NHS provision generally
  - Promoting a comprehensive health service
  - Medical, nursing and care services
  - Weak duty to provide services
  - Difficulty in challenging NHS on grounds of lack of resources
  - Challenging the NHS on grounds other than resources
  - Consultation about changes to, or closure of, services
- General medical practitioners
- Health overview and scrutiny committees and LINKs
- Funded nursing care in nursing homes
- Community health services in care homes and people's own homes
- NHS charges for services
- Hospital discharge
  - Community Care (Delayed Discharges) Act 2003
  - Delayed discharge assessment notices
  - Duty of social services authority on receipt of assessment notice
  - Discharge notices
  - Liability to make delayed discharge payments
  - Delayed discharge criteria, decision-making and reviews
  - Refusal of patient to leave hospital
  - Interim accommodation after discharge: suitability for person's needs
- Joint working between local authorities and the NHS
- Intermediate care

- Community equipment
  - Examples of community equipment
  - Community equipment in care homes
  - Continence products
  - Retail model for equipment: 'transforming community equipment services'
- Single assessment process
- Care Programme Approach for people with mental health needs
  - Shortcuts in joint working in mental health

SUMMARY

NHS services in the community, together with admission to and discharge from hospital, play a crucial role in community care.

The NHS has a general duty to provide services under the NHS Act 2006. However, the duty is weak and difficult to enforce. Unlike in the case of local social services authorities, there is no clear rule that once an individual person's 'eligible need' has been identified, then it must be met. The NHS can nearly always argue a lack of resources as a legal defence for not providing services. This comes as a surprise to many people. However, it is this legal rule that accounts, of course, for the widespread and seemingly inevitable rationing imposed by the NHS and for the sometimes gross local deficiencies to be found in less glamorous services – particularly those for chronically sick and older people.

Nonetheless, in recent years, the NHS has on occasion been checked (a) by the courts in relation to consultation about closure of services, and to excessively rigid or logically incoherent policies, and (b) by the health service ombudsman in relation to NHS continuing health care.

NHS PROVISION GENERALLY

The main duties in the NHS Act 2006 underpinning the provision of health services are as follows. They lie on the Secretary of State, but are generally delegated to NHS primary care trusts, who delegate further to NHS trusts (acute hospital and other trusts).[1]

---

1   *NHS Act 2006*, ss.1, 3, 7, 19. And see: SI 202/2375. *NHS (Functions of Strategic Health Authorities and Primary Care Trusts and Administration Arrangements) (England) Regulations 2002.*

PROMOTING A COMPREHENSIVE HEALTH SERVICE

The Secretary of State must continue the promotion in England of a comprehensive health service designed to secure improvement (a) in the physical and mental health of the people of England, and (b) in the prevention of, diagnosis and treatment of illness. For that purpose, the Secretary of State must provide or secure the effective provision of services.[2]

The Secretary of State has the power (a) to provide such services as he or she considers appropriate for the discharge of any duty in the NHS Act 2006, and (b) to do any other thing to facilitate, or which is conducive or incidental to, the discharge of such a duty.[3]

MEDICAL, NURSING AND CARE SERVICES

The Secretary of State must, to such extent as he or she 'considers necessary to meet all reasonable requirements', provide (italics added):

(a) *hospital accommodation* or other accommodation for the purpose of any service provided under the Act

(b) *medical, dental, ophthalmic, nursing and ambulance services*

(c) other services for the care of pregnant women, women who are breastfeeding and young children as he or she considers appropriate as part of the health service

(d) other services or facilities for the *prevention of illness*, the care of people *suffering from illness* and the *aftercare* of people who have suffered from illness – such as he or she considers are appropriate as part of the health service

(e) such other services or facilities as are required for the *diagnosis and treatment* of illness.[4]

WEAK DUTY TO PROVIDE SERVICES

The Act is vague. It does not contain a detailed list of services, such as continence services, community nursing, stoma care, palliative care, respite care, physiotherapy, speech and language therapy, physiotherapy, chiropody. Even in respect of those services that are mentioned, such as medical or nursing, the duty is a general one only. It has been

---

2   *NHS Act 2006*, s.1.
3   *NHS Act 2006*, s.2.
4   *NHS Act 2006*, s.3.

characterised by the courts as a target duty only, barely amenable to enforcement by individual patients.[5]

DIFFICULTY IN CHALLENGING NHS ON GROUNDS OF LACK OF RESOURCES

The generality of the duties contained in the NHS Act 2006 means that the NHS has been highly successful in defending legally the non-provision of services owing to lack of resources. Such legal cases have involved, for instance, orthopaedic patients waiting years for treatment,[6] children with heart conditions not getting operations[7] and a child with leukaemia being denied potentially lifesaving treatment.[8]

CHALLENGING THE NHS ON GROUNDS OTHER THAN RESOURCES

The NHS has been legally challenged more successfully on grounds other than lack of resources.

For instance, central government guidance must be properly taken account of by the NHS. A failure to do so in relation to drug treatment for multiple sclerosis meant that the health authority had acted unlawfully.[9] In another court case, a health authority misinterpreted unlawfully its responsibilities to provide continuing health care.[10] The NHS has also been successfully challenged because of rigid policies that 'fetter its discretion' in relation to, for instance, gender reassignment surgery[11] or cancer drugs.[12] The health service ombudsman, too, has faulted blanket policies concerning powered wheelchairs, breast reduction surgery,[13] homoeopathic treatment[14] and growth hormone treatment.[15]

5   *R v Inner London Education Authority (ILEA), ex p Ali* [1990] 2 ALR 822.

6   *R v Secretary of State for Social Services, ex p Hincks* [1980] 1 BMLR 93, Court of Appeal.

7   *R v Central Birmingham Health Authority, ex p Collier* (1998) unreported, Court of Appeal; *R v Central Birmingham Health Authority, ex p Walker* [1987] 3 BMLR 32, Court of Appeal.

8   *R v Cambridge Health Authority, ex p B* [1995] 6 MLR 250, Court of Appeal.

9   *R v North Derbyshire Health Authority, ex p Fisher* [1998] 8 MLR 327.

10 *R v North and East Devon Health Authority, ex p Coughlan* (1999) 2 CCLR 285, Court of Appeal.

11 *R v North West Lancashire Health Authority, ex p G,A,D* (1999) 2 CCLR 419, Court of Appeal.

12 *R(Otley) v Barking and Dagenham Primary Care Trust* [2007] EWHC Admin 1927; *R(Gordon) v Bromley NHS Primary Care Trust* [2006] EWHC 2462 Admin; *R(Rogers) v Swindon NHS Primary Care Trust* [2006] EWCA Civ 392.

13 *Epsom and St Helier NHS Trust 2001* (E.559/99–00). And: *North Essex Health Authority 2001* (E.1099/00–01). Both cases in: Health Service Ombudsman (2001) HC 278–I. *Selected Investigations Completed August–November 2000.* London: TSO.

14 *East Sussex, Brighton and Hove Health Authority 1999* (E.1316/98–99). In: Health Service Ombudsman (1999) HC 19. *Investigations Completed April–September 1999.* London: TSO.

15 North Essex Health Authority 2003 (E.1033/01–02. In: Health Service Ombudsman (2003) HC 787. *Selected Investigations Completed December 2002–March 2003.* London: TSO.

CONSULTATION ABOUT CHANGES TO, OR CLOSURE OF, SERVICES

A number of legal cases followed widespread proposed and actual cutbacks and changes to health services from 2005 onwards.[16] The cases involved both the duty to consult about such changes under s.242 of the NHS Act 2006,[17] and the common law rules about consulting fairly. These cases have involved, for instance, independent-sector treatment centres replacing local NHS services,[18] closing minor injuries units and day hospitals,[19] shutting community hospital beds,[20] closing community hospitals altogether,[21] and contracting out general practitioner services to the private sector.[22] These cases have had limited success; even when the NHS bodies concerned have been found to have acted unlawfully, the courts have been slow to provide a substantial remedy (such as ordering the reopening of a service).[23]

GENERAL MEDICAL PRACTITIONERS

Community-care policy guidance states that, as a matter of good practice, general practitioners (GPs) will wish to make a full contribution to community care assessments. It reminds local authorities that GPs are not always best placed to assess on behalf of a local authority, since GPs have a personal duty and relationship with their patients; in which case, local authorities might wish other practitioners to act in that capacity.[24]

Under their own contractual terms with primary care trusts, GPs have to provide a consultation at the request of a person at least 75 years old who has not had such a consultation in the previous 12 months. GPs must refer patients for other services provided under the NHS Act 2006; this would include not just health services but also community care services provided by local authorities under s.254 and schedule 20 of the Act.[25]

---

16 Mandelstam, M. (2006) *Betraying the NHS: Health Abandoned.* London: Jessica Kingsley Publishers, Chapter 5.

17 Formerly s.11 of the *Health and Social Care Act 2001*.

18 *R(Fudge) v South West Strategic Health Authority* [2007] EWCA Civ 803.

19 *R(Compton) v Wiltshire Primary Care Trust* [2009] EWHC 1824 Admin.

20 *R(Morris) Trafford Healthcare NHS* [2006] EWHC Admin 2334.

21 *R v North and East Devon Health Authority, ex p Pow* (1998) 39 BMLR 77.

22 *Smith v North Eastern Derbyshire Primary Care Trust and Secretary of State* [2006] EWCA Civ 1291, Court of Appeal.

23 *R(Morris) Trafford Healthcare NHS* [2006] EWHC Admin 2334.

24 Department of Health (1990) *Community in the Next Decade and Beyond: Policy Guidance.* London: DH, paras 3.47–3.48.

25 SI 2004/291. *NHS (General Medical Services Contracts) Regulations 2004*, r.15, schedules 5 and 6.

HEALTH OVERVIEW AND SCRUTINY COMMITTEES AND LINKS

Local health overview and scrutiny committees scrutinise and review local health-service provision. The committees are made up of democratically elected local councillors; this is in contrast to the members of NHS trust and primary care trust boards, who are not directly accountable to the local population. These committees have the power to make referrals to the Secretary of State, who in turn has the power to appoint an Independent Reconfiguration Panel to investigate and review local NHS proposals.[26]

A further theoretical safeguard in the NHS decision-making process is that of public involvement more generally. In 2008, legislation replaced what used to be called public and patient involvement forums (PPIFs) with Local Involvement Networks (LINKs). Their function is to be involved in commissioning, provision and scrutiny of local health and social care services. They have power to make recommendations and a right to receive a response from the local NHS.[27]

FUNDED NURSING CARE IN NURSING HOMES

People in nursing homes who are not eligible for NHS continuing health care (see below) are eligible to have some of their fee paid by the NHS to cover the funded nursing care they need.

The basic rules are set out in directions, which create a duty. They state that if the PCT thinks a person in a care home may require nursing care, then it must carry out an assessment. Before doing so, the PCT must decide whether to carry out an NHS continuing health care assessment. If the PCT decides that the person does need funded nursing care, it has to pay a flat-rate contribution (currently £106.30 per week) to the care home. In case of urgency, the PCT can temporarily provide nursing care to a person without having carried out an assessment.[28]

Guidance emphasises that this funded nursing-care decision is separate from the decision about a person's eligibility for NHS continuing health care.[29] A decision about the latter should be made first. A challenge to a

---

26 *NHS Act 2006*, s.244; SI 2002/3048. *Local Authority (Overview and Scrutiny Committees Health Scrutiny Functions) Regulations 2002;* and *Local Government Act 2000*, s.21.

27 *Local Government and Public Involvement in Health Act 2007*, ss.221–226, 230–231. And: SI 2008/528. *Local Involvement Networks Regulations 2008.*

28 Department of Health. *NHS (Nursing Care in Residential Accommodation) (England) Directions 2007.* As amended by the *NHS (Nursing Care in Residential Accommodation) (Amendment) (England) Directions 2009.* London: DH.

29 Department of Health (2009) *National Framework for NHS Continuing Health Care and NHS-funded nursing care.* London: DH, Annex D.

decision about NHS-funded nursing care can be made under the same review process as for NHS continuing health care.[30]

COMMUNITY HEALTH SERVICES IN CARE HOMES AND PEOPLE'S OWN HOMES

Guidance states that residents of care homes, whether or not they are nursing homes, should have access to professional advice about incontinence, as well as incontinence products. Chiropody services and other therapies (such as physiotherapy, occupational therapy, speech and language therapy and podiatry) should be made available on a similar basis to their provision in other settings such as people's own homes.[31] Such a statement is of limited value, since such services delivered to people's own homes are highly variable and there is, indeed, no clear duty to provide them at any particular level.

NHS CHARGES FOR SERVICES

The NHS does not have the same duties and powers as local social services authorities to make charges for services. Some items are charged for if specified in legislation – for example (and subject to various exemptions), equipment and drugs prescribed by general practitioners, or wigs, surgical brassières, and spinal supports provided to hospital outpatients.[32] But everything else, both services and equipment must be provided free of charge.[33] Legally, this would seem to be straightforward. However, some NHS bodies have for many years made legally dubious charges – for instance, for chiropody appliances and orthopaedic footwear.[34]

In addition, the NHS has made sometimes controversial[35] though lawful charges for non-clinical services, such as car parking and the use of telephones on hospital wards. This is permissible under income generation legislation.[36] Central government in England has come under pressure to curb these highly unpopular and arguably exploitative schemes.

---

30 Department of Health (2009) *National Framework for NHS Continuing Health Care* ... paras 150–151.

31 Department of Health. *NHS-funded Nursing Care: Practice Guide (Revised) 2009.* London: DH, paras 44.

32 SI 2000/620. *NHS (Charges for Drugs and Appliances) Regulations 2000.* Made under the *NHS Act 2006*, s.172.

33 *NHS Act 2006*, s.1.

34 HSO W.226/91–92. In: Health Service Commissioner (1992) HC 32. *1st Report 1991–1992.* London: HMSO. And: *North Bristol NHS Trust 2000* (E.2041/98–99) in: Health Service Ombudsman. HC 541–I. *Summaries of Investigations Completed October 1999–March 2000.* London: TSO.

35 House of Commons Health Committee (2006) *NHS charges.* HC 815–I. London: TSO.

36 *Health and Medicines Act 1988.*

HOSPITAL DISCHARGE

When leaving hospital, some people's needs are complicated. Consideration of many factors is often required, including physical ability, mental ability and attitude, informal carers, social and environmental factors and financial situation. There are sometimes many arrangements to make.

The pressure on NHS acute hospitals and their beds is such that people continue to be discharged with undue haste by acute hospitals. One reason for this is that many slower stream, rehabilitation and recuperation beds have been closed over the past few years – together with such beds in community hospitals.[37] This can result in people being discharged inappropriately back to their own home or to care homes, where their rehabilitation and recuperation needs are inadequately met. Another consequence is immediate readmission to hospital; such readmission rates are reported to be increasing.[38]

The overall problem is made significantly worse when acute hospitals operate excessively high bed-occupancy levels, leading to reduced care standards, problematic infection control and premature hospital discharge – for instance, waking patients up in the middle of the night and sending them home.[39] The health service ombudsman has continued over the years to investigate poor discharge practices, these cases representing almost certainly the tip of an iceberg.

COMMUNITY CARE (DELAYED DISCHARGES) ACT 2003

The Community Care (Delayed Discharges) Act 2003 imposes financial penalties on local social services authorities if they are deemed to be responsible for delays in people's discharge from hospital – even if that delay is beyond their practical control.

The rules under the Act apply in practice to acute care only. They do not cover paying patients, maternity care, mental health care, palliative care, intermediate care, recuperation or rehabilitation. (Mental health care is defined as psychiatric services or other services for preventing, diagnosing or treating illness where a consultant psychiatrist is primarily responsible for those services).[40]

---

37 British Geriatric Society (2007) *Rehabilitation Beds Report on the Second England Council Survey.* London: BGS.
38 Taylor, A. 'The war on the wards.' *Community Care,* 13 December 2007, p.12.
39 Bond, A. 'Hospital hit by bed crisis.' *East Anglian Daily Times,* 22 December 2007.
40 SI 2003/2276. *Delayed Discharges (Mental Health Care) (England) Order 2003.*

The rules are set out in some detail because they can be useful in order to protect people from inappropriate, and sometimes almost reckless, discharge from hospital. Hospital social workers, for example, are well accustomed to using them to protect patients.

DELAYED DISCHARGE ASSESSMENT NOTICES
A 'section 2' notice must be given by the NHS requesting the local authority to assess the patient, if discharge without community care services is likely to be unsafe. The notice can be given up to eight days prior to a hospital admission but no less than two days before the date of proposed discharge. The patient and, if reasonably practicable, the carer must be consulted before the notice is given.

The notice must be withdrawn in certain circumstances if (a) the NHS considers it would no longer be safe to discharge the person, (b) it considers the person needs NHS continuing care, (c) it considers safe discharge will not be achieved without further community care services provided than those already proposed, (d) the patient's proposed treatment has been cancelled or postponed.

The assessment notice must be in written form and dated. It must include likely date of discharge, a statement that the patient and carer have been consulted – and that the NHS has considered whether or not to provide NHS continuing health care, and the result of that decision. It must refer to whether the patient has objected to the notice, and also to the name of the liaison person between hospital and social services. The minimum assessment period is set at two days; a notice issued after 2 pm is treated as having been issued on the following day. Sundays and public holidays do not count as part of the minimum interval; they are also excluded for the purpose of issuing an assessment notice.[41] Directions separately place a duty on the NHS to take a view about continuing care, before serving an assessment notice on the local authority.[42]

DUTY OF SOCIAL SERVICES AUTHORITY ON RECEIPT OF ASSESSMENT NOTICE
On receipt of the s.2 assessment notice, the local authority must assess the person's needs for community care services necessary for a safe

41 *Community Care (Delayed Discharges) Act 2003*, ss.2–3. SI 2003/2277. *Delayed Discharges (England) Regulations 2003*.
42 Department of Health. *Delayed Discharges (Continuing Care) Directions 2009*. London: DH.

discharge. After consulting the NHS, it must decide what services to provide. It must also assess any informal carer under the Carers and Disabled Children Act 2000 – and decide, again after consulting the NHS, what services to provide. However, the duty to assess the carer only arises if the carer has requested an assessment.

The local authority must keep under review both the patient's and the carer's needs in relation to the services required for safe discharge. The local authority can alter its decision in the light of changed circumstances following the assessment.[43]

DISCHARGE NOTICES

The NHS must consult social services before deciding what services to provide on discharge, and give social services notice of the proposed date of discharge. However, it cannot do this unless it has also issued an assessment notice. Discharge notices issued after 2 pm on Fridays or 5 pm on other days are treated as having been issued on the following day. The minimum interval between the giving of the notice and the discharge day is one day. Sundays and public holidays in England and Wales do not count as part of the minimum interval.[44]

LIABILITY TO MAKE DELAYED DISCHARGE PAYMENTS

If the end of the agreed discharge date is reached and the patient has not been discharged because social services has failed (a) to carry out an assessment or to take a decision about what services are required, or (b) has not made available community care or carer's services it had agreed to provide, then social services must make a payment for each day of delayed discharge. If the reason for the delayed discharge is not solely due to the social services authority's failure, then the reimbursement duty does not arise.

The delayed discharge period begins with the day after (from 11 am) the discharge day and ends no later than the day of actual discharge.[45] Therefore, at the minimum a charge could not be made until three days after an assessment (and discharge) notice had been given – and at the minimum 48 hours could be specified for assessment and arranging of services.[46]

---

43   *Community Care (Delayed Discharges) Act 2003*, s.4.

44   *Community Care (Delayed Discharges) Act 2003*, s.5; SI 2003/2277. *Delayed Discharges (England) Regulations 2003*.

45   *Community Care (Delayed Discharges) Act 2003*, s.6.

46   HSC 2003/009. Department of Health. *Community Care (Delayed Discharges) Act 2003*, paras 76–79.

DELAYED DISCHARGE CRITERIA, DECISION-MAKING AND REVIEWS

A person can challenge a discharge decision by means of the review panels set up to deal with continuing care decisions. In case of dispute between public authorities, those authorities may apply to the strategic health authority for the appointment of a panel. Legal proceedings cannot be brought until such a panel has made a recommendation.[47]

REFUSAL OF PATIENT TO LEAVE HOSPITAL

Sometimes people, judged fit for discharge, refuse to leave hospital. Guidance states that patients do not have the right to stay in a hospital bed if they no longer need the care,[48] but is silent about what to do. In practice, the NHS might require an eviction order – as obtained by Barnet Primary Care Trust when a patient refused to leave for some two years.[49]

INTERIM ACCOMMODATION AFTER DISCHARGE: SUITABILITY FOR PERSON'S NEEDS

Because of the delayed discharge rules, people are more likely to be placed by local authorities temporarily in interim, or 'step-down', accommodation, so as to avoid reimbursement charges payable to the NHS.

For some, such interim accommodation might be suitable and more beneficial than remaining in hospital. For others, it might harm their physical and mental welfare. Even moving from ward to ward or hospital to hospital can be detrimental, let alone a premature move to different accommodation altogether.

However, even an interim placement must legally meet a person's needs under the NHS and Community Care Act 1990. Guidance states that it must be based 'solely' on the person's assessed need, and must sustain or improve independence; otherwise the person should remain in hospital and the local authority should reimburse the NHS.[50]

---

47 *Community Care (Delayed Discharges) Act 2003*, s.9; SI 2003/2277. *Delayed Discharges (England) Regulations 2003.*
48 HSC 2003/009. Department of Health. *Community Care (Delayed Discharges) Act 2003*, para 96.
49 'Man ordered out of hospital bed', *BBC News* 6 March 2006. Available at http://news.bbc.co.uk/1/hi/england/london/4779472.stm, accessed on 22 March 2007.
50 HSC 2003/009. Department of Health. *Community Care (Delayed Discharges) Act 2003*, para 97.

JOINT WORKING BETWEEN LOCAL AUTHORITIES AND THE NHS

Legislation gives the NHS and local social services authorities the power to pool budgets and to delegate their functions to one another.[51] There are various other provisions contained in the NHS Act 2006 and other legislation that permit joint arrangements. These include the NHS making payments to local authorities to assist the latter to carry out social services functions – and vice versa.[52] In addition, other policies relevant to joint working are to be found in guidance. These include policies on intermediate care, a 'single assessment process' for older people, community equipment services and the Care Programme Approach (CPA) for people with mental health needs.

There would seem to be obvious benefits in joint working, in terms of greater cohesion of services and perhaps avoidance of duplication of assessment and documentation. However, sometimes it seems that joint working is used as a cover to erode people's statutory rights; for example, when the social services functions are neither understood nor properly adhered to in joint mental health teams (see below).

INTERMEDIATE CARE

Regulations legally define intermediate care as a 'structured programme of care provided for a limited period of time to assist a person to maintain or regain the ability to live in his home'. They also prohibit local authorities from charging for intermediate care (residential or non-residential) services for up to six weeks.[53] The health care element of intermediate care must anyway be free of charge.[54]

In practice, increasing numbers of local authorities appear to be renaming their intermediate care services (e.g. 'reablement services') and then charging even within the six-week period. However, if the re-labelled service continues to fit the definition of intermediate care in the regulations and guidance, then this trend would appear to be yet one more of the potentially unlawful shortcuts discussed in Chapter 2. Department of Health practice guidance states that intermediate care should be:

---

51 *NHS Act 2006*, s.75. Formerly in: *Health Act 1999*, s.31.
52 *NHS Act 2006*, ss.76, 256.
53 SI 2003/1196. *Community Care (Delayed Discharges) (Qualifying Services) (England) Regulations 2003*.
54 *NHS Act 2006*, s.1.

(a) for people who would otherwise face unnecessarily prolonged hospital stays or inappropriate admission to acute inpatient care, long-term residential care or NHS continuing inpatient care

(b) provided on basis of comprehensive assessment, resulting in a structured individual care plan involving active therapy, treatment or opportunity for recovery

(c) planned with an outcome of maximising independence and typically enabling people to live at home

(d) time limited, normally no longer than six weeks and frequently as little as one to two weeks

(e) involve cross-professional working, with a single assessment framework, single professional records and shared protocols.

The guidance lists the following as constituting intermediate care services: rapid response teams, acute care at home, residential rehabilitation, supported hospital discharge (including home care support), day rehabilitation.[55]

COMMUNITY EQUIPMENT

The provision of community equipment services – by both local authorities and the NHS – has long been recognised as inadequate.[56] The Department of Health finally issued guidance in 2001. It stated that local authorities should increase the number of people benefiting from community equipment services by 50 per cent and integrate local authority and NHS community equipment services by March 2004.[57] The policy was called 'integrating community equipment services' (ICES).

EXAMPLES OF COMMUNITY EQUIPMENT

The guidance referred to home-nursing equipment such as pressure relief mattresses and commodes, together with daily living equipment such as shower chairs and raised toilet seats. It also listed minor adaptations (e.g. grab rails, lever taps, improved lighting), sensory impairment equipment (e.g. liquid-level indicators, hearing loops, assistive listening devices,

55 Department of Health (2009) *Intermediate Care: Halfway Home.* London: DH, pp. 3, 8.
56 Audit Commission (2000) *Fully Equipped: The Provision of Equipment to Older or Disabled People by the NHS and Social Services in England and Wales.* London: Audit Commission.
57 HSC 2001/008; LAC(2001)13. Department of Health. *Community Equipment Services.* London: DH.

flashing doorbells), communication aids, wheelchairs for short-term loan and telecare equipment (e.g. fall alarms, gas escape alarms, health-state monitoring devices).[58] The list is non-exhaustive; the assessed needs of a service user might call for other types of equipment.

In addition is a new development referred to as 'telecare'. This signifies preventative technology to enable people to remain in their own homes with assistance from a range of new technologies, including alarms, sensors and monitors, backed up by control centres. Department of Health guidance warns that telecare should be a part of wider care planning and that the risks of social isolation need to be taken into account.[59] In other words, telecare should not be seen as a cheap option for abandoning people.

COMMUNITY EQUIPMENT IN CARE HOMES

Regulations under the Care Standards Act 2000 (in the future, under the Health and Social Care Act 2008) are vague about equipment in care homes. Even the more detailed national minimum standards made under the Act refer sparingly to grab rails, other aids, hoists, assisted toilets and baths, communication aids such as loop systems and storage areas for equipment.[60]

Disputes regularly arise about responsibility for particular items of equipment. Department of Health guidance states that: 'care homes providing nursing care are expected to be fit for purpose, which, in the main, means they will have in place basic handling, mobility, and lifting equipment and adaptations. There may be some situations where they will need to draw on the resources of the local community equipment service.'

It differentiates between equipment that the care home should be providing for the generality of residents, and equipment that is bespoke for an individual resident. The latter should not fall to the care home but instead to the local authority or NHS.[61]

CONTINENCE PRODUCTS

Guidance states that people in care homes should be provided with continence products, subject to an assessment of need. More specifically,

---

58 Department of Health (2001) *Guide to Integrating Equipment Services*. London: DH.
59 LAC(2006)5. Department of Health. *Preventative technology Grant 2006/07–2007/08*. London: DH. See also: Department of Health (2005) *Building Telecare in England*. London: DH.
60 Department of Health (2003) *Care Homes for Older People: National Minimum Standards*. London: DH.
61 Department of Health. *NHS-funded Nursing Care: Practice guide (Revised) 2009*. London: DH, paras 49.

it states that for people receiving NHS-funded nursing care in a care home, the NHS should provide the continence products for them or at least the pay the care home to cover their provision.[62]

RETAIL MODEL FOR EQUIPMENT: 'TRANSFORMING COMMUNITY EQUIPMENT SERVICES'

The Department of Health has recently formulated a 'retail model' of equipment provision called 'transforming community equipment services' (TCES). The policy is based on no new legislation or legally authoritative guidance; its main elements are as follows. In practice, some local authorities and primary care trusts are operating this model, others are not.

First, people will receive assessment of needs as normal. Second, for people with complex needs or with a need for large items of equipment (such as hoists), local authorities and the NHS will remain directly responsible for provision. Third, the model covers mainly low-cost equipment, listed on a 'national tariff'. Fourth, people assessed as eligible for such equipment will be given prescriptions to be used in the independent sector. Fifth, before this happens, people should be offered rehabilitation where appropriate – which may make equipment unnecessary. Sixth, those assessed as ineligible will be advised to buy their own equipment.[63]

SINGLE ASSESSMENT PROCESS

In 2002, the Department of Health issued guidance on a 'single assessment' process for older people.[64] In summary, it urged local authorities and the NHS to work jointly to assess older people. It set out four different levels of assessment corresponding to complexity of people's needs: contact, overview, specialist and comprehensive. (The guidance is due to be revised.)[65]

---

62 Department of Health. *NHS-funded Nursing Care: Practice Guide (Revised) 2009.* London: DH, paras 51.
63 Care Services Improvement Partnership (2007) *Transforming Community Equipment and Wheelchair Services Programme.* London: CSIP.
64 HSC 2002/001; LAC(2002)1. Department of Health. *Guidance on the Single Assessment Process for Older People.* London: DH.
65 Department of Health (2009) *Common Assessment Framework for Adults: A Consultation on Proposals to Improve Information Sharing Around Multi-Disciplinary Assessment and Care Planning.* London: DH.

CARE PROGRAMME APPROACH FOR PEOPLE WITH MENTAL HEALTH NEEDS

The CPA applies primarily to the NHS. It is based on good practice guidance; although the courts have stated this is not the source of NHS duties and powers towards people with a mental disorder.[66]

It concerns provision of higher levels of support for people with mental health problems who (a) have a wide range of needs relating to a number of services, or (b) are at most risk. It does not affect aftercare duties owed to people under s.117 of the Mental Health Act 1983, although such people should be included within the CPA framework.[67]

SHORTCUTS IN JOINT WORKING IN MENTAL HEALTH

The guidance on CPA urges joint working between the NHS and local authorities.[68] However, such working can result in shortcuts being taken and to the undermining of statutory duties, particularly those pertaining to social services.[69] The courts have warned against collapsing social services duties to assess and provide services into NHS guidance that is not necessarily consistent with social services rules.[70] Department of Health guidance has issued the same warning about not equating eligibility for community care services with eligibility for CPA.[71]

66 *K v Central and North West London Mental Health NHS Trust, and Kensington and Chelsea Royal London Borough Council* [2008] EWHC 1217 QB.

67 Department of Health (2008) *Refocusing the Care Programme Approach: Policy and Positive Practice Guidance.* London: DH.

68 Department of Health (2008) *Refocusing the Care Programme Approach* ... Executive Summary.

69 Commission for Social Care Inspection (2008) *Cutting the Cake Fairly.* London: CSCI, 2008, para 3.24–3.30.

70 *R(HP) v Islington London Borough Council* [2004] EWHC Admin 07.

71 Department of Health (2008) *Refocusing the Care Programme Approach* ... p.13.

CHAPTER 14

NHS continuing health care

- Background to NHS continuing health care
  - Funding nursing care
- What does NHS continuing health care mean?
- Procedural rules about continuing care
  - Continuing care and rules about discharge from an acute hospital
  - Continuing care assessment rules for primary care trusts
- NHS continuing health care: guidance
- Primary health need
  - Nature, intensity, complexity or unpredictability of health care needs
- NHS is the decision-maker about a primary health need
- Avoiding pitfalls in the decision-making process
  - Providing continuing care in all settings
  - Current successful management does not preclude continuing health care needs
  - Proper recording of decision
  - Eligibility decision should not be affected by financial gate-keeping by primary care trusts
- End-of-life eligibility
- Legal and ombudsman cases indicative of continuing care
- NHS continuing health care for people in their own homes
- Challenging continuing care decisions
  - Convening a review panel at strategic health authority level
  - Limited remit of panels
  - Local dispute resolution between NHS and local authority
  - Ombudsmen
  - Judicial review

SUMMARY

If people have a continuing 'primary health need', then they are entitled to what is called 'NHS continuing health care'. This means that the NHS arranges and pays for people's health care, nursing care, personal care and accommodation in hospital, in a care home, in a hospice – and for their health, nursing and personal care in their own home. The advantages to patients of receiving this care – both in terms of the nature of the care itself and financially (the care might otherwise have to be paid for) – can be considerable. However, the rules have long since been far from clear and are applied by the NHS variably and restrictively.

In summary, the result has been unedifying. The policy of central government of running down NHS provision of such care over the past twenty years has been surreptitious and underhand; it has not been properly and publicly explained, debated and scrutinised. It has been characterised by arbitrary, inconsistent, unaccountable, maladministrative and sometimes unlawful decision-making by the NHS. Local authorities, too, have largely acquiesced in this and been drawn into unlawfully charging people huge sums of money – involving their savings and sometimes their houses. And it has affected both highly vulnerable people in various stages of serious and complex illness, disability and dying – and their often distraught and anxious families.

For all these reasons, the rules – to the extent that they can be made sense of at all – are set out in some detail in this chapter.

BACKGROUND TO NHS CONTINUING HEALTH CARE

NHS decisions about continuing care have been criticised consistently by the health service ombudsman for some sixteen years. The ombudsman has exposed the fact that the Department of Health's policy has not been clear and fair. Many people have been wrongly charged for care, with probably tens of thousands of people over this period having had to spend their savings and sell their homes.

Largely as a result of the health service ombudsman's efforts, the Department of Health was forced to authorise significant repayment of money to individual patients and their families from 2004 onwards – in the region of £180–200 million, averaging £90,000 per person wrongly charged.[1] It published new guidance in 2007 (revised in

---

1   Womack, S. 'Elderly care blunders cost NHS £180m.' *Daily Telegraph*, 13 February 2008.

2009) in the form of a 'national framework', together with three sets of 'directions'. These were designed, ostensibly, to clarify the rules; it is not clear that this has happened.

FUNDING NURSING CARE

For people in nursing homes, there is a distinction between NHS continuing health care (attracting full NHS funding) and 'funded nursing care'. The latter, the funded nursing care, involves the NHS paying £106.30 per week towards a person's registered nursing care in nursing homes. The NHS does not cover the rest of the care home fee, which will be paid either by people themselves or the local authority if people have too little money to pay (see Chapter 5).

WHAT DOES NHS CONTINUING HEALTH CARE MEAN?

NHS continuing health care can apply in a range of settings. In hospital, care home or hospice, it means the NHS arranges and funds the whole package – accommodation, and all health, nursing and personal care.

In a person's own home, it means the NHS funds not just health and nursing care, but also personal care. The advantages are that people may, in principle, receive a higher standard and input of health care and rehabilitation, and that they will not be charged for the personal care (the health and nursing care would anyway be free), which would be normally chargeable under community care legislation.

PROCEDURAL RULES ABOUT CONTINUING CARE

The Department of Health has passed 'directions' imposing specific duties on the NHS.

CONTINUING CARE AND RULES ABOUT DISCHARGE FROM AN ACUTE HOSPITAL

Before the NHS gives a local authority notice to assess a person with a view to discharge from an acute hospital bed, it must first take reasonable steps to ensure that an NHS continuing care assessment is carried out. This is where it appears to the NHS body – in consultation, where it considers this appropriate, with the local social services authority – that the patient may have a need for such care. The NHS must (italics added):

(a) *consult with the patient* and, where it considers it appropriate, the patient's carer

(b) use a *'needs checklist' for screening (if it wishes to screen)* to decide whether to undertake an assessment for NHS continuing health care

(c) *inform the person about the decision* and make a record in the patient's notes

(d) ensure a *multi-disciplinary assessment*

(e) ensure that a *'decision support tool'* is completed and informs the decision about whether a person has a primary health need (signifying NHS responsibility)

(f) *decide that a person is eligible for NHS continuing health care* if it has decided that the person has a primary health need.

The NHS must consider whether – if the person is going into a care home – his or her *needs are more than incidental or ancillary* to the provision of the accommodation, or are of a nature beyond that which a social services authority could be expected to provide. If either of these two conditions is satisfied, then the NHS body must conclude that the person has a primary health need.

However, if an appropriate clinician (a) decides a person has primary health need arising from a *rapidly deteriorating condition*, (b) decides that the condition may be entering a terminal phase, and (c) has completed a fast-track pathway tool, then the person *automatically qualifies* for NHS continuing health care.

The NHS body must also, where a continuing care assessment has been carried out, notify the person in writing and make a record in the person's notes. It must, where the decision is that the person is ineligible, inform the person (or somebody acting on his or her behalf) that he or she can apply for a review. This could relate to how, procedurally, the NHS body reached its decision or to how it applied the primary health need test.[2]

CONTINUING CARE ASSESSMENT RULES FOR PRIMARY CARE TRUSTS

A second set of rules place obligations generally on NHS primary care trusts (PCTs), strategic health authorities (SHAs) and local social services authorities.

---

2   Department of Health. *Delayed Discharges (Continuing Care) Directions 2009*. London: DH.

They state that a PCT must take reasonable steps to ensure that an NHS continuing care assessment is carried out. The procedure is then similar to that followed by NHS trusts, under the directions set out immediately above. The PCT must, as far as is reasonably practicable, consult with the social services authority, before making a decision about a person's eligibility for continuing care. The local authority must, as far as is reasonably practicable, provide advice and assistance to the PCT. Nothing in the rules affects the duty of a local authority to assess under s.47 of the NHS and Community Care Act 1990.

Any dispute between the PCT and local authority about eligibility for NHS continuing health care, or about the contribution of either to a jointly funded package of care, should be resolved through an agreed local dispute-resolution procedure

Each SHA must establish a panel, including an independent chairman, to consider reviews of continuing care decisions involving either procedure followed by a PCT or NHS trust or how they applied the primary health need test. The SHA has a power, not a duty, to convene the review panel.[3]

NHS CONTINUING HEALTH CARE: GUIDANCE

In addition to the two sets of directions set out above, which provide a procedural framework, further Department of Health guidance elaborates. This includes a national framework,[4] a decision support tool,[5] a checklist for screening purposes,[6] a fast-track pathway tool,[7] and guidance on NHS-funded nursing care.[8] In addition, the Association of Directors of Adult Social Services (ADASS) and the Local Government Association have issued guidance of their own.[9]

PRIMARY HEALTH NEED

Directions state that NHS continuing health care 'means a package of care arranged and funded solely by the health service for a person aged 18 or over to meet physical or mental health needs which have arisen as a

---

3   Department of Health. *NHS Continuing Healthcare (Responsibilities) Directions 2009*. London: DH.
4   Department of Health (2009) *National Framework for NHS Continuing Health Care and NHS-funded Nursing care*. London: DH.
5   Department of Health (2009) *Decision Support Tool for NHS Continuing Healthcare*. London: DH.
6   Department of Health (2009) *NHS Continuing Healthcare Checklist*. London: DH.
7   Department of Health (2009) *Fast-track Pathway Tool for NHS Continuing Healthcare*. London: DH.
8   Department of Health. *NHS-funded Nursing Care: Practice Guide (Revised) 2009*. London: DH.
9   Association of Directors of Adult Social Services (2007) *Commentary and Advice for Local Authorities on the National Framework for NHS Continuing Healthcare and NHS-funded Nursing Care*. London: ADASS, LGA.

result of illness'.[10] Guidance confirms that this actually means 'disability, accident or illness' and involves care provided over an extended period of time.[11]

The key legal test for NHS continuing health care is whether the person has a 'primary health need'.[12] This means that the person's need is primarily a health need.[13] The courts have held that a person is only ineligible for NHS continuing health care in a nursing home if the nursing required is (a) no more than incidental or ancillary to the provision of residential accommodation, which the local authority is under a duty to provide, and (b) is not of a nature beyond which a local authority, whose primary responsibility is to provide social services, could be expected to provide.[14]

The ADASS guidance points out that for local authorities to fund more than what is incidental or ancillary – that is, to fund a person with nursing needs that are a major, rather than a lesser, part of what is being provided – is consequently unlawful.[15]

The overall question then is whether a person has a primary health need; the guidance issued by the Department of Health is merely a means to this legal end. The courts have ruled that failure to understand this will make a decision unlawful,[16] although they may give primary care trusts the benefit of the doubt.[17]

If the NHS does decide to meet a person's need on the basis of NHS continuing health care status, it only has to do so in the most cost-effective way.[18]

NATURE, INTENSITY, COMPLEXITY OR UNPREDICTABILITY OF HEALTH CARE NEEDS

The Department of Health guidance states that certain characteristics of need may indicate NHS continuing health care. These are nature, intensity, complexity and unpredictability. It states that 'each of these characteristics may, in combination or alone, demonstrate a primary

---

10   Department of Health. *Delayed Discharges (Continuing Care) Directions 2009*. London: DH.
11   Department of Health (2009) *National Framework* ... para 8. Illness is defined in s.275 of the *NHS Act 2006* to include injury, disability or disorder/disability of mind.
12   Department of Health (2009) *National Framework* ... para 25.
13   *R v North and East Devon Health Authority, ex p Coughlan* (1999) 2 CCLR 285, Court of Appeal; *R(Grogan) v Bexley NHS Care Trust* [2006] EWHC 44.
14   Department of Health (2009) *National Framework* ... para 26.
15   Association of Directors of Adult Social Services (2007) *Commentary* ... p.11.
16   *R(Grogan) v Bexley NHS Care Trust* [2006] EWHC 44.
17   *R(Green) v South West Strategic Health Authority* [2008] EWHC 2576 Admin.
18   *R(S) v Dudley Primary Care Trust* [2009] EWHC 1780 Admin (permission to apply for judicial review).

health need, because of the quality and/or quantity of care required'.[19] Any one characteristic could therefore be sufficient. It is not necessary for a person's condition, for example, to be unstable or unpredictable if it were complex. However, the courts have pointed out that 'care needs are not [by definition] health care needs if they are by nature complex, intense or unpredictable, since they have to be health care needs in the first place'.[20]

To assist decision-making, the Department of Health has published a decision support tool, which covers 'domains' of need: behaviour, cognition, communication, psychological and emotional needs, mobility, nutrition (food and drink), continence, skin and tissue viability, breathing, drug therapies and medication (symptom control), altered states of consciousness, other significant needs. People are scored against these domains, as to whether their needs are priority, severe, high, moderate or low. A sufficiently high score, such as one priority, two severe domains, one severe and perhaps a few highs, will indicate continuing health care status.[21]

If applied to the claimant in the *Coughlan* case (see below), it is probable that the tool would not (in most PCTs) produce a decision to award continuing care. Yet, the courts have held that she most certainly did have continuing care status in law. This might suggest that the tool is not consistent with the approach taken by the Court of Appeal in that case.

NHS IS THE DECISION-MAKER ABOUT A PRIMARY HEALTH NEED

Ultimately, a legal challenge by a local authority (or by anybody else) to an NHS decision – for example, that a person's needs were not of the primary health variety – is not without difficulty. In one case involving a local authority challenge against the NHS, the Court of Appeal was unenthusiastic. It more or less stated that most if not all the cards lay with the NHS – and that local authority decision-making could in principle not hold its own against the NHS in the continuing care context.[22]

19 Department of Health (2009) *National Framework* ... paras 28–29.
20 *R(St Helens Borough Council) v Manchester Primary Care Trust* [2008] EWCA Civ 931.
21 Department of Health (2009) *Decision Support Tool* ... paras 21, 32.
22 *R(St Helens Borough Council) v Manchester Primary Care Trust* [2008] EWCA Civ 931.

AVOIDING PITFALLS IN THE DECISION-MAKING PROCESS

Department of Health guidance sets out further key points to remedy common defects in NHS decision-making.

PROVIDING CONTINUING CARE IN ALL SETTINGS

The guidance states that NHS continuing health care may be provided by PCTs in any setting (including, but not only, a care home, hospice, person's own home). Thus, eligibility decisions should not be based on setting of care;[23] the health service ombudsman has frequently found fault in this regard.[24]

CURRENT SUCCESSFUL MANAGEMENT DOES NOT PRECLUDE CONTINUING HEALTH CARE NEEDS

The guidance states that a continuing care decision should not be based on:

(a) whether or not the person's needs are currently being successfully managed

(b) use or not of NHS employed staff to provide care

(c) need for/presence of 'specialist staff' in care delivery

(d) existence of other NHS-funded care, or

(e) any other input-related (rather than needs-related) rationale.[25]

This answers the health service ombudsman's criticism in the past that the requirement of 'specialist' intervention was unduly restrictive.[26] Similarly, the question of current successful management, or use or not of NHS staff, was dealt with by the ombudsman in a case when a wife was successfully providing expert care for her husband (who had dementia) at home. Despite the reluctance of the NHS, the ombudsman held that he qualified for continuing health care.[27]

---

23 Department of Health (2009) *National Framework* ... para 47.

24 *Dorset Health Authority 2003* (E.208/99–00): in Health Service Ombudsman (2003) *NHS Funding for Long Term Care*. London: TSO. *Shropshire Health Authority 2003a* (E.2119/01–02): in Health Service Ombudsman (2003) HC 787. *Selected Investigations Completed December 2002–March 2003*. London: TSO. *Cambridgeshire Health Authority 2004* (E.22/02–03) in: Health Service Ombudsman (2004) HC 704. *Selected Investigations Completed October 2003–March 2004*. London: TSO. *North Worcestershire Health Authority 1995* (E.264/94–95): in Health Service Commissioner HC 11. *Selected Investigations Completed April to September 1995*. London: HMSO.

25 Department of Health (2009) *National Framework* ... para 49.

26 Health Service Ombudsman (2004) *Annual Report 2003–04*. London: TSO, para 19.

27 *Cambridgeshire Health Authority 2004* (E.22/02–03) in: Health Service Ombudsman (2004) HC 704. *Selected Investigations Completed October 2003–March 2004*. London: TSO.

PROPER RECORDING OF DECISION

The guidance states that the decision-making process should be 'accurately and fully recorded'.[28]

ELIGIBILITY DECISION SHOULD NOT BE AFFECTED BY FINANCIAL GATE-KEEPING BY PRIMARY CARE TRUSTS

The guidance states that financial issues should not affect the outcome of decisions about eligibility for continuing care. PCT panels should not play a financial monitoring role and should not contain finance officers. Multi-disciplinary team recommendations should be overturned by panels only exceptionally and with clearly articulated reasons. Eligibility decisions should not delay treatment or appropriate care. Assessment should always consider further potential for rehabilitation, and the risks and benefits of change of location should be considered before a move takes place.[29]

END-OF-LIFE ELIGIBILITY

Guidance states that there should be a fast-track process for people rapidly deteriorating. It also states that that one or more of the characteristics of need (nature, intensity, complexity or unpredictability) 'may well apply to those people approaching the end of their lives, and eligibility should always be considered'.[30]

The Department of Health has accordingly published guidance in the form of a fast-track assessment tool, to help clinicians make decisions if a person has a rapidly deteriorating condition that may be entering a terminal phase, and has an increasing level of dependency. Directions stipulate that completion of this tool by an appropriate clinician automatically triggers NHS continuing health care eligibility (see above).

The guidance tool states that strict time limits, in terms of length of life remaining, should not be imposed to establish eligibility.[31] The ADASS guidance is more specific, suggesting that people with a prognosis of 12 weeks to live or less, should receive NHS funding.[32]

---

28 Department of Health (2009) *National Framework* ... para 71.
29 Department of Health (2009) *National Framework* ... paras 48, 56, 79.
30 Department of Health (2009) *National Framework* ... paras 28–29.
31 Department of Health (2009) *Fast-track Pathway Tool* ... para 4.
32 Association of Directors of Adult Social Services (2007) *Commentary* ... p.13.

LEGAL AND OMBUDSMAN CASES INDICATIVE OF CONTINUING CARE

Department of Health guidance states that PCTs should be aware of legal and health service ombudsman cases that have indicated eligibility for NHS continuing health care. Although it stresses the importance of individual assessment, the implication is that PCTs should give serious consideration to awarding NHS continuing health care to patients who are similar to those in indicative cases – of which the most important has been the *Coughlan* case. The following are but three examples, including *Coughlan*, in which continuing care status was established:

Substantial nursing care

A man was doubly incontinent, could not eat or drink without assistance, could not communicate, had a kidney tumour, cataracts in both eyes and occasional epileptic fits. There was no dispute that when he was discharged he did not need active medical treatment but did need 'substantial nursing care'. Failure to provide continuing care was unreasonable and a failure in the duty to provide a service for a highly dependent person.[33]

More than incidental and ancillary

A woman, who had been badly injured in a road traffic accident, was described as tetraplegic, doubly incontinent, requiring regular catheterisation, partially paralysed in respiratory function, subject to problems attendant on immobility and also to recurrent headaches caused by an associated neurological condition. She required regular nursing input but not active medical treatment. Her nursing needs were held to be more than just 'incidental or ancillary' to the provision of accommodation, and were not of a nature that social services could be expected to provide.[34]

Eligibility for continuing care without input by a registered nurse

One health service ombudsman case involved the care at home by a woman (and personal assistants) of her husband, who had Alzheimer's disease. One of the grounds on which the NHS had held that he was not continuing health care status was that he was not receiving regular care from registered nurses. Two of the senior staff involved in continuing care decisions (the manager and director, both nurses) stated that the wife was not providing nursing care, since nursing qualifications and skills could not be self-taught and took many years to acquire. Therefore the care being given by the wife could not be highly professional.

Yet both an independent medical consultant and the consultant psychiatrist involved disagreed with this view; they said that the severity of the man's condition meant he had health care needs 'well beyond' anything that the average care worker was competent to deal with. The consultant psychiatrist also gave the view that the care was being provided

---

33 *Leeds Health Authority 1994* (E.62/93–94): in Health Service Commissioner (1994) *Failure to Provide Long Term NHS Care for Brain-damaged Patient*. London: HMSO.

34 *R v North and East Devon Health Authority, ex p Coughlan* (1999) 2 CCLR 285, Court of Appeal.

in a professional manner, and was equal to, if not superior to, the care the husband would have received on an NHS dementia ward. Indeed, the 'atmosphere was not one that could be replicated in a continuing care ward'.[35]

There are number of others cases also indicative of NHS continuing health care.[36]

NHS CONTINUING HEALTH CARE FOR PEOPLE IN THEIR OWN HOMES

Guidance states that NHS continuing health care in a person's own home means that the 'NHS funds all the care and support that is required to meet their assessed health and care needs. Such care may be provided either within or outside the person's home, as appropriate to their assessment and care plan'.[37]

The ADASS guidance states that the NHS should be responsible for all health and personal care services, as well as associated social-care services essential to daily living, such as equipment provision, routine and incontinence laundry – and daily domestic tasks such as food preparation, shopping, washing up, bed making, etc. Whereas local authorities might still assist in terms of adapting the property, essential parenting activities, access to leisure or other community facilities, carer services including additional general domestic support.[38]

However, it is arguable that home adaptations, directly linked to a person's continuing health care needs, should be funded by the NHS as well. Certainly, there is a precedent for this; longstanding Department of Health guidance makes clear that adaptations needed directly for renal dialysis in a person's home, should be an NHS responsibility – including, if necessary, a separate room and direct water supply.[39]

---

35 *Cambridgeshire Health Authority 2004* (E.22/02–03) in: Health Service Ombudsman (2004) HC 704. *Selected Investigations Completed October 2003–March 2004.* London: TSO.

36 E.g. *Berkshire Health Authority 2003* (E.814/00–01) in: Health Service Ombudsman (2003) *NHS Funding for Long Term Care.* London: TSO. Also: HSO W.478/89–90) in: Health Service Commissioner (1991) HC 482. *2nd Report 1990–1991.* London: HMSO. Also: North Worcestershire Health Authority 1995 (E.264/94–95) in: Health Service Commissioner (1995) HC 11. *Selected Investigations Completed April to September 1995.* London: HMSO.

37 Department of Health (2009) *National Framework* ... Annex A.

38 Association of Directors of Adult Social Services (2007) *Commentary* ... p.7.

39 HSC(IS)11. Department of Health and Social Security (1974) *Services for Chronic Renal Failure.* London: DHSS. Also: HSG(93)48. Department of Health. *Home Dialysis Patients: Costs of Metered Water for Home Dialysis.* London: DH.

CHALLENGING CONTINUING CARE DECISIONS

The directions (above) state that PCTs should inform people about how to apply for a review of a decision about NHS continuing health care or about NHS-funded nursing care (in a care home). Guidance states that PCTs should deal promptly with review requests, usually by convening a panel. Normally, the time between referral for a full consideration of need, and communication of the decision to the patient, should not exceed two weeks. However, if referral has taken place and NHS funding is still ongoing, the process may take longer. Where a longer period is required for valid and unavoidable reasons, time-scales should be clearly communicated to the person and their carers.[40]

CONVENING A REVIEW PANEL AT STRATEGIC HEALTH AUTHORITY LEVEL

If the person remains dissatisfied following a PCT review, the case should be referred to the Strategic Health Authority's Independent Review Panel (IRP). The convening of an SHA review panel is a discretion, not a duty.[41] The panel reports back to the SHA, which must then give notice to the applicant and the PCT or NHS trust. The health service ombudsman has in the past stated that such discretion should be exercised properly.[42]

The guidance states that the IRP must gather and scrutinise all available and appropriate evidence, compile/identify needs, involve the individual and carer as far as possible, fully record panel deliberations, and reach clear and evidenced decisions that explain the rationale. There should be consistency between the panel deliberations, the recommendations and the decision letter. The IRP function is advisory but the PCT should accept its recommendations in all but exceptional circumstances.[43]

LIMITED REMIT OF PANELS

The directions state that the review can be requested in relation to the procedure adopted by the PCT, or to the way in which the primary health criterion has been applied. Guidance makes clear, however, that the IRP procedure does not apply to challenges to the content

---

40 Department of Health. *National Framework* ... paras 79–84.

41 Department of Health. *NHS Continuing Healthcare (Responsibilities) Directions 2007*. London: DH.

42 *Herefordshire Health Authority 1999* (E.1321/98–99): in Health Service Ombudsman (1999) HC 19. *Investigations Completed April–September 1999*. London: TSO.

43 Department of Health (2009) *National Framework* ... para 158.

of eligibility criteria, the type and location of NHS-funded continuing care services on offer, the content of any alternative care package that has been offered, or treatment or any other aspect of services being received. Complaints about these issues should be made through the ordinary NHS complaints procedure.[44]

Beyond the IRP, the case can then be referred to the health service ombudsman.

LOCAL DISPUTE RESOLUTION BETWEEN NHS AND LOCAL AUTHORITY

Guidance states that where a dispute arises between different NHS bodies or between the local authority and the PCT, there should be an agreed local dispute-resolution process. The dispute should not delay the provision of the care package.[45] The NHS may, at least in some circumstances, be expected to continue funding until the review procedure is complete.[46]

OMBUDSMEN

If people are dissatisfied with the SHA's review panel decision, then they can try to take the dispute further to the health service ombudsman, and likewise if the dispute has proceeded through the ordinary complaints procedure.

A complaint might sometimes lie against the local authority if it has not taken steps to assist a person with a continuing care application to the NHS and instead has stood back and watched the family wrongly pay nursing home fees. The local ombudsman found maladministration in such a case.[47]

JUDICIAL REVIEW

Judicial review cases can be taken against the NHS (or local authorities) by or on behalf of a patient, or even by a local authority against the NHS (although the courts do not generally welcome this step).[48]

---

44 Department of Health (2009) *National Framework* ... Annex E.

45 Department of Health (2009) *National Framework* ... para 161.

46 *Barnet Healthcare NHS Trust 2000* (E.33/99–00): in Health Service Ombudsman (2000) HC 541–I. *Summaries of Investigations Completed October 1999–March 2000*. London: TSO.

47 *Hertfordshire County Council 2003* (00/B/16833).

48 *R(St Helens Borough Council) v Manchester Primary Care Trust* [2008] EWCA Civ 931.

CHAPTER 15

Mental capacity, human rights, and disability discrimination

- Mental capacity
  - Five key principles about mental capacity
  - Mental capacity test and best interests
  - Powers of attorney, deputies, advance health care decisions
  - Advocates
  - Wilful neglect or ill-treatment
- Human rights
  - Public authorities
  - Right to life (article 2)
  - Inhuman or degrading treatment (article 3)
  - Deprivation of liberty (article 5)
  - Right to respect for private and family life (article 8)
  - Justification for interference (article 8): accordance with the law
  - Necessity of interference (article 8)
  - Interference for a particular purpose under article 8
- Disability discrimination
  - Definition of disability
  - Provision of goods and services to the public
  - Less favourable treatment
  - Justifying less favourable treatment or not taking reasonable steps

- Management, letting, etc. of premises
- Education
- Disability equality duty

SUMMARY

In addition to community care and NHS legislation, yet further legislation affects health and social care. This includes the Mental Capacity Act 2005, the Human Rights Act 1998 and the Disability Discrimination Act 1995.

The Mental Capacity Act 2005 puts in place a number of provisions designed both to empower and protect people who do, or might, lack mental capacity to make particular decisions for themselves – about, for example, where they should live, who they should have contact with, what medical treatment they should have, and whether they can manage their own affairs.

The Human Rights Act 1998 brought the European Convention on Human Rights directly into United Kingdom law. It is designed to protect citizens from the excesses of public bodies (including local authorities and the NHS) – for instance, not to be subjected to inhuman or degrading treatment, not to be deprived arbitrarily of liberty, and not to have one's private life unduly interfered with. Human rights have played a part in social care and health care legal cases, but have perhaps had a lesser impact than was expected by some people.

The Disability Discrimination Act 1995 creates various duties designed to prevent discrimination against disabled people. These include duties in relation to the provision of goods and services (including social care and health care), the letting out and management of premises, and a specific duty on public bodies to promote disability equality.

MENTAL CAPACITY

The importance and complexity of people's mental capacity in health and social care has become more widely recognised with the implementation of the Mental Capacity Act 2005 – and the increasing numbers of people with dementia and severe learning disabilities. It is beyond the scope of this book to cover this legislation, other than the following summary.

FIVE KEY PRINCIPLES ABOUT MENTAL CAPACITY

The Act sets out five key principles that are about both empowering people as well as protecting them. These are that:

(a) people should be assumed to have capacity to take particular decisions, unless there is a balance of evidence suggesting they do not

(b) people should be given all practicable assistance to help them take decision for themselves

(c) the fact that a person with an impairment in the functioning of mind or brain makes an unwise decision does not necessarily mean they lack capacity

(d) an intervention for somebody lacking capacity must be made in his or her best interests

(e) consideration must be given to using the least restrictive intervention to achieve the purpose in issue.[1]

MENTAL CAPACITY TEST AND BEST INTERESTS

The Act then sets out the rules about a number of matters, including how to define and test for lack of capacity. It lists how to ascertain the 'best interests' of a person lacking capacity. The Act provides legal protection for people who provide care and treatment for a person lacking capacity, so long as they have done so reasonably and in good faith. At the same time the Act prohibits excessive restraint of a person.[2]

It contains separate rules about going beyond restraint and consequently depriving a person of his or her liberty. Such rules are required, because particular concern and difficulty has surrounded the circumstances in which people lacking mental capacity are deprived of their liberty in hospitals or care homes.[3] The Act now contains safeguards whereby people lacking capacity can only be deprived of their liberty either by the Court of Protection, or by a local authority or primary care trust granting a 'standard authorisation', following careful assessment of a number of matters, including mental capacity, best interests, etc. In some cases, care homes or hospitals can grant urgent, but only very temporary, authorisations.[4]

---

1   *Mental Capacity Act 2005*, s.1.
2   *Mental Capacity Act 2005*, ss.2–6.
3   *R v Bournewood Community and Mental Health NHS Trust, ex p L* [1998] 1 CCLR 390, House of Lords.
4   *Mental Capacity Act 2005*, ss. 4A–4B, schedules 1A and A1.

POWERS OF ATTORNEY, DEPUTIES, ADVANCE HEALTH CARE DECISIONS

The Act also covers the law of 'necessaries' (about when a contract is enforceable even if a person lacks capacity). It covers lasting power of attorney. This is when a person (the 'donor') with capacity creates a power authorising an attorney in the future to take not only financial decisions but also health and welfare decisions for the donor, if and when the latter loses capacity to take those decisions. Parallel with this, the Court of Protection can intervene in matters of capacity – not only in financial, but also in health and welfare, matters – by means of orders, the appointment of deputies and the resolution of disputes or uncertainties.[5]

The Act clarifies the law about advance decisions or 'living wills' as they are sometimes called. They involve a person with capacity, stipulating in advance their refusal of specified medical treatment, in case at the relevant time (when treatment is required) he or she lacks the capacity to do so directly.[6]

ADVOCATES

The Act also underpins a statutory independent mental-capacity advocacy (IMCA) service, which means that in certain circumstances local authorities and NHS bodies have an obligation to instruct an advocate before a decision is made.[7]

WILFUL NEGLECT OR ILL-TREATMENT

A new offence of wilful neglect or ill-treatment of a person lacking capacity, with a maximum sentence of five years in prison, is contained in the Act.[8]

HUMAN RIGHTS

The Human Rights Act 1998 embeds the European Convention on Human Rights 1998 into United Kingdom law. The 1998 Act is the vehicle; the main rights themselves lie within the Convention. Particularly relevant in health and social care are:

- article 2 (right to life) of the Convention

---

5   *Mental Capacity Act 2005*, ss.7–23.
6   *Mental Capacity Act 2005*, ss.24–26.
7   *Mental Capacity Act 2005*, ss.35–41.
8   *Mental Capacity Act 2005*, s.44.

- article 3 (right not to be subjected to torture or to inhuman and degrading treatment)

- article 5 (right not to be arbitrarily deprived of liberty)

- article 8 (right to respect for private and family life, home and correspondence)

- article 14 (right not to be discriminated against).

The Act is about maintaining a balance between individual autonomy and freedom on the one hand, and interference by the State on the other. Human rights cases can only be taken against public bodies, or bodies carrying out functions of a public nature.

PUBLIC AUTHORITIES

The Human Rights Act applies to public authorities only. A public authority is defined to include, in addition to obvious bodies such as local authorities, any person in respect of whom some functions are of a public nature (s.6).

The courts held that this rule excluded independent health and social care providers from having human rights obligations towards users of their services[9] – except in the case of compulsory mental health detention.[10] The government then decided to change the legislation, which now states that care homes carry out functions of a public nature – and are thus subject to the Human Rights Act 1998 – but only in relation to residents placed by local authorities under ss.21 and 26 of the National Assistance Act 1948. This amending legislation is, however, limited. It does not extend human rights protection to people who are:

(a) placed in an independent care home by the NHS

(b) placed by local authorities and/or the NHS in an independent care home under s.117 of the Mental Health Act 1983

(c) are self-funding residents who have their own contractual arrangements with the independent care home, or

(d) who receive services in their own home from independent domiciliary care agencies.[11]

---

9   *YL v Birmingham City Council* [2007] UKHL 27.

10   *R v Partnerships in Care Ltd, ex p A* [2002] EWHC Admin 529.

11   *Health and Social Care Act 2008*, s.145.

RIGHT TO LIFE (ARTICLE 2)

Article 2 states: 'Everyone's right to life shall be protected by law'. In the context of community care, it has been argued unsuccessfully in a number of cases concerning the closure of care homes.[12] However, in one case about care provided in a person's own home, the judge suggested that leaving disabled people to drown in a bath, because staff might injure themselves effecting a rescue, could engage article 2.[13] In another case, it was unsuccessfully argued that the criminal law concerning assisted suicide breached article 2.[14] Forcible treatment under the Mental Health Act may raise matters issues under article 2, as well as under articles 3 and 8.[15]

INHUMAN OR DEGRADING TREATMENT (ARTICLE 3)

Article 3 states: 'No one shall be subjected to torture or to inhuman or degrading treatment or punishment'. Inhuman or degrading treatment means that the ill-treatment in question must reach a minimum level of severity, and involve actual bodily injury or intense physical or mental suffering. Degrading treatment could occur if it 'humiliates or debases an individual showing a lack of respect for, or diminishing, his or her human dignity or arouses feelings of fear, anguish or inferiority capable of breaking an individual's moral and physical resistance'.[16]

In one community care case, a local authority failed to find suitably adapted accommodation for a disabled woman for two years; she lived for this period in squalid and undignified conditions. The judge considered whether article 3 had been breached. However, in the end he found a breach of article 8 only.[17] In another, the court held that if manual-handling policies meant that care staff would leave disabled people for hours sitting in their own bodily waste or on the lavatory, article 3 might be engaged. On the other hand, the hoisting of disabled people was not to be regarded as inherently degrading; whether or not it was would depend on the particular circumstances.[18]

---

12 E.g. *R(Haggerty) v St Helens Metropolitan Borough Council* [2003] EWHC Admin 803.
13 *R(A&B, X&Y) v East Sussex County Council (no.2)* [2003] EWHC Admin 167.
14 *Pretty v United Kingdom* [2002] 2 FCR 97, European Court of Human Rights.
15 *R v Responsible Medical Officer Broadmoor Hospital, ex p Wilkinson* [2001] EWCA Civ 1545.
16 *Pretty v United Kingdom* [2002] 2 FCR 97, European Court of Human Rights.
17 *R(Bernard) v Enfield London Borough Council* [2002] EWHC Admin 2282.
18 *R(A&B, X&Y) v East Sussex County Council (no.2)* [2003] EWHC Admin 167.

DEPRIVATION OF LIBERTY (ARTICLE 5)

Article 5 states that everyone has a right to liberty and security and that nobody should be deprived of it, except in limited circumstances and, even then, only in accordance with procedures prescribed by law. A number of more detailed rules then follow.

Article 5 was held to have been breached by the European Court of Human Rights in the case of informal, compliant but incapacitated mental-health patients kept in hospital.[19] In a later case, a local authority was held to have deprived a mentally incapacitated person of his liberty, without proper legal procedure, when it placed him in a care home and refused to let him return to his own home.[20]

Such cases have led to the amendment of the Mental Capacity Act 2005 and to the introduction of a formal system of authorising the deprivation of liberty of people lacking capacity, and who do not come under the Mental Health Act 1983 (which carries its own safeguards against arbitrary detention).

RIGHT TO RESPECT FOR PRIVATE AND FAMILY LIFE (ARTICLE 8)

Article 8 states that everyone has the right to respect for his private and family life, his home and his correspondence. It goes on to say that there should be no interference unless it is in accordance with the law and is necessary in a democratic society. In addition, the interference must be:

(a) in the interests of national security, public safety or the economic well-being of the country

(b) for the prevention of disorder or crime

(c) for the protection of health or morals, or

(d) for the protection of the rights and freedom of others.

In a number of cases, the courts have stated that private life encompasses a person's physical and psychological integrity.[21]

A local authority was held to have breached article 8 when it failed to deal with the daily living and accommodation needs of a severely disabled woman living in dire domestic circumstances.[22]

---

19 *HL v United Kingdom* (2004) 40 EHRR 761, European Court of Human Rights.
20 *JE v DE and Surrey County Council* [2006] EWHC Fam 3459.
21 E.g. *Botta v Italy* (1998) Case no. 21439/93, European Court of Human Rights.
22 *R(Bernard) v Enfield London Borough Council* [2002] EWHC Admin 2282.

Likewise a health authority, when it breached an explicit promise about accommodation for a disabled woman.[23] And the courts have held that article 8 can apply to manual-handling issues in terms of dignity, hoisting and other transfers, and the disabled person's participation in the life of the community.[24]

However, the courts have emphasised that article 8 is not a broad brush to enforce provision of welfare benefits.[25] Even so, they drew the line at the failure of a local authority to assess properly a 95-year-old woman, when deciding that she should not return from hospital to the care home she had been living in but instead had to go to another. The authority had failed to weigh up the effect of its decision on her physical and psychological integrity; it had thus breached article 8.[26]

JUSTIFICATION FOR INTERFERENCE (ARTICLE 8): ACCORDANCE WITH THE LAW

If a local authority is to justify, under article 8.2, the interference with the right to respect under 8.1, the first ground to be satisfied is that the interference be in accordance with the law. This means the relevant domestic law, other than the Human Rights Act 1998.

In one case involving the decision to close a local authority care home, the judge stated that he could not envisage any circumstances in which the council could act compatibly with the common law and its other statutory obligations and yet be in breach of human rights, whether under articles 2, 3 or 8.[27] In another case, concerning the lawfulness of offering a care home place instead of accommodation in the community, the court stated that community care legislation was broad, humane and took account of needs including family and private life. Therefore reference to article 8 of the Convention took the case no further.[28]

On the other hand, when a local authority breached article 8 by not arranging suitably adapted accommodation for a disabled woman,[29] any justification in terms of the authority's action being in 'accordance with

---

23   *R v North and East Devon Health Authority, ex p Coughlan* (1999) 2 CCLR 285, Court of Appeal.

24   *R(A&B, X&Y) v East Sussex County Council (no.2)* [2003] EWHC Admin 167.

25   *R(Anufrijeva) v Southwark London Borough Council* (2003) 6 CCLR 415, Court of Appeal.

26   *R(Goldsmith) v Wandsworth London Borough Council* [2003] EWHC Admin 2941; [2004] EWCA Civ 1170, Court of Appeal.

27   *R(Cowl) v Plymouth City Council* [2001] EWHC Admin 734.

28   At High Court stage: *R(Khana) v Southwark London Borough Council* (2000) unreported; [2001] EWCA Civ 999, Court of Appeal.

29   *R(Bernard) v Enfield London Borough Council* [2002] EWHC Admin 2282.

the law' would have failed. This was because the judge had anyway found the local authority to be in breach of the relevant domestic legislation, namely s.21 of the National Assistance Act 1948.

NECESSITY OF INTERFERENCE (ARTICLE 8)
In addition to being in accordance with domestic law, the interference must be 'necessary in a democratic society'. That is, the intervention must be proportionate; a sledgehammer should not be used to crack a nut. So, if a local authority is, for instance, proposing to remove a person lacking capacity from their own home, it would have to explain why this was really necessary – usually in terms of risk – rather than choosing a lesser option.

INTERFERENCE FOR A PARTICULAR PURPOSE UNDER ARTICLE 8
Finally, assuming accordance with the law and proportionality, any interference must also be for a purpose specified under article 8. For instance, one purpose listed is economic well-being of the country. Inevitably, this has arisen in community care, since so many disputes are ultimately about money. Under community care legislation, a duty to meet to people's needs has only to be discharged in the most cost-effective manner. Thus, the economic well-being of Walsall justified that local authority's decision to close a care home and place residents elsewhere.[30] Similarly, closure of a day centre, and transfer of attendees elsewhere, could be justified with reference to the economic well-being of the local authority area of Bromley.[31]

Other purposes justifying interference are the protection of health and the protection of the rights and freedoms of others. When the NHS wished to close an accommodation lodge for people with mental health problems, the courts stated that any rights under article 8 were inextricably bound up with the trust's obligation to provide medical care for the benefit of the claimants. Furthermore, the closure would benefit other members of the community to whom the trust owed a duty and who enjoyed the rights and freedoms that the trust had to respect.[32]

---

30 *R(Rowe) v Walsall Metropolitan Borough Council* (2001) unreported (leave to apply for judicial review). See also: *R(Dudley) v East Sussex County Council* [2003] EWHC Admin 1093.
31 *R(Bishop) v Bromley London Borough Council* [2006] EWHC 2148 Admin.
32 *R v Brent, Kensington and Chelsea and Westminster NHS Trust, ex p C* [2002] EWHC 181.

DISABILITY DISCRIMINATION

The Disability Discrimination Act 1995 (DDA) is divided into various sections covering employment, the provision of goods and services, management of premises, education and public transport. The DDA sits alongside the Race Relations Act 1976 and the Sex Discrimination Act 1975.

The government intends to repeal all three Acts and subsume discrimination law into a single Equality Act. This will include age discrimination not only in relation to workplace discrimination (at present under the Employment Equality (Age) Regulations 1996), but also – for the first time – in respect of the provision of goods and services. The government has conceded that there is a 'significant amount of evidence that older people are treated in a discriminatory way by those providing goods and services, including health and social care'.[33]

DEFINITION OF DISABILITY

Disability is defined under the DDA as physical or mental impairment that has a substantial and long-term adverse effect on the person's ability to carry out normal day-to-day activities.[34]

PROVISION OF GOODS AND SERVICES TO THE PUBLIC

Providers of goods and services to the public must not discriminate against disabled people by refusing to provide, or not providing, a service that is provided to others, or providing it on worse terms or at a lower standard than it would be provided for others.[35]

They must also not discriminate by failing to make reasonable adjustments to practices, policies and procedures, or in respect of physical features – or failing to take reasonable steps to provide auxiliary aids or services. The result of this failure to make reasonable adjustments must be to make it impossible or unreasonably difficult for the disabled person to use the service.[36]

For instance, when a wheelchair passenger could not change platforms at a particular railway station, the courts found him

---

33 Lord Privy Seal, Leader of the House of Commons, Minister for Women and Equality (2008) *Framework for a Fairer Future: The Equality Bill.* Cm 7431. London: Government Equalities Office.
34 *Disability Discrimination Act 1995*, s.1. And: SI 1996/1455. *Disability Discrimination (Meaning of Disability) Regulations 1996.*
35 *Disability Discrimination Act 1995*, s.19.
36 *Disability Discrimination Act 1995*, ss.20–21.

discriminated against, because the railway company had not provided a taxi to get him from one platform to another by road.[37]

LESS FAVOURABLE TREATMENT

A provider of services discriminates by treating a person less favourably than others – on grounds relating to his or her disability – where that less favourable treatment cannot be justified. Thus, what would otherwise be discrimination is capable of being justified on particular grounds (s.20).

Less favourable treatment could be in comparison with non-disabled people, or with people with other disabilities. For instance, providing assistance to get from the airport check-in to the plane – free of charge for disabled people already owning a wheelchair, but at a charge for less disabled people – constituted discrimination.[38] However, in a case involving local authority charging for non-residential services, the court held that disabled people had to pay not because they were disabled but because they had the money to pay.[39]

JUSTIFYING LESS FAVOURABLE TREATMENT OR NOT TAKING REASONABLE STEPS

Less favourable treatment, or the failure to take reasonable steps, can be justified on grounds of:

(a) health and safety

(b) the incapacity of the person to enter into a contract

(c) the service provider otherwise being unable to provide the service to the public

(d) enabling the service provider to provide the service to the disabled person or other members of the public

(e) a greater cost being applied to the service, because it reflects a greater cost to the provider (but not the costs incurred by making reasonable adjustments).[40]

The justification can only be made out if (a) the service provider believed that one of these defences applied, and (b) it was reasonable for the provider to believe this. If the defence is made out, then there

---

37   *Roads v Central Trains* [2004] EWCA Civ 1541.
38   *Ross v Ryanair* [2004] EWCA Civ 1751, Court of Appeal.
39   *R v Powys County Council, ex p Hambidge (no.2)*(2000) LGR 564, Court of Appeal.
40   *Disability Discrimination Act 1995*, s.20.

is no discrimination under the Act. For instance, prohibiting staff from hazardous manual handling to change a school pupil's incontinence pads was not discriminatory because of the health and safety issues at stake.[41] However, pleading health and safety without having carried out a proper risk assessment will be fairly hopeless – as happened when a boy was excluded from a school trip on grounds of his diabetes.[42]

MANAGEMENT, LETTING, ETC. OF PREMISES

The DDA contains a number of provisions affecting residential premises and possession orders,[43] including landlords' giving of permission for adaptations and making reasonable adjustments for tenants.

A number of cases have reached the courts concerning the attempts of landlords to evict tenants with mental health problems. The tenants argued in these cases that their errant behaviour (the grounds of possession sought) was linked to their disability and thus constituted discrimination. These cases culminated in a House of Lords case in which the Law Lords redressed the balance, which they felt had tipped too far against landlords. They made two key points in respect of (a) the comparison to be made between the disabled tenant and other tenants, and (b) the landlord's knowledge of the tenant's disability and motivation for seeking eviction.[44]

EDUCATION

The Disability Discrimination Act 1995 applies to education at all levels.[45] In the case of further and higher education, there are duties on the bodies responsible for educational institutions. These must not discriminate by treating disabled students less favourably for a reason relating to their disability, or by failing to make reasonable adjustments so as to avoid putting disabled students at a substantial disadvantage (subject to justification).

DISABILITY EQUALITY DUTY

Public bodies have a disability equality duty. They must have due regard to the need to:

(a) eliminate discrimination that is unlawful under the Act

---

41   *K v X Grammar School Governors* [2007] EWCA Civ 165.
42   *White v Clitheroe Royal Grammar School* (2002) Claim BB 002640, Preston County Court.
43   *Disability Discrimination Act 1995*, ss.22–24.
44   *Malcolm v Lewisham London Borough Council* [2008] UKHL 43.
45   *Disability Discrimination Act 1995*, ss.28R–28T.

(b) eliminate harassment of disabled people

(c) promote equality of opportunity between disabled people and other people

(d) take steps to take account of people's disabilities, even if that means treating disabled people more favourably

(e) encourage the participation of disabled people in public life.[46]

'Have regard to' does not mean that the public body has actually to achieve these aims.

When a local authority was making its eligibility criteria for community care services stricter, the s.49A duty was not drawn to the attention of councillors at two crucial meetings. The decision was therefore unlawful and would have to be retaken.[47] When a local authority sought to replace live-in sheltered housing wardens with 'floating' wardens, it was held to have acted unlawfully. This was because it did not take properly into account the effect of this policy on disabled people.[48] And when the National Institute for Clinical Excellence issued guidance about the use of certain drugs for people with Alzheimer's disease, the courts held it had failed to take account of its duties under s.49A of the DDA.[49]

However, the outcome was different when a local authority provided support for a disabled person to go to university but judged his toileting needs there to be less than critical or substantial, and therefore not eligible for help. The court held in effect that s.49A was not enough to overrule the application of eligibility criteria – even though the assessment had not spelt out that the DDA had been taken account of.[50] Likewise, there was no breach s.49A when a local authority consulted over whether to re-impose financial charges for non-residential community care services or instead restrict eligibility for services. Either way, disabled people would suffer, but it was in the context of a decision (not under challenge in the case) that had already been taken by the council, to reduce its council tax by 3 per cent.[51]

---

46 *Disability Discrimination Act 1995*, s.49A.
47 *R(Chavda) v Harrow London Borough Council* [2007] EWHC 3064 Admin.
48 *R(Boyejo) v Barnet London Borough Council* [2009] EWHC 3261 Admin.
49 *Eisai Ltd v National Institute for Health and Clinical Excellence* [2008] EWCA Civ 438.
50 *R(M) v Birmingham City Council* [2009] EWHC 688 Admin.
51 *R(Domb) v Hammersmith & Fulham London Borough Council* [2009] EWCA Civ 941.

CHAPTER 16

Health and safety at work legislation, and the law of negligence

- Health and safety at work legislation
  - Duties to protect employees and non-employees
  - Reasonable practicability in health and safety: weighing up people's needs and staff safety
  - Manual handling: proportionate, balanced decision-making
  - Contracting out services: responsibilities of health or social care commissioner
- Negligence

SUMMARY

It is beyond the scope of this book to set out in any detail health and safety at work legislation and the common law of negligence. Nonetheless, such matters do impinge on community care. For example, manual handling continues to pose numerous problems for both staff and users of services – about whether a hoist is required, how many carers are needed to move a person, etc. And, in respect of negligence cases against the NHS and local authorities, the courts continue to struggle to decide when to make findings of liability, and when to protect such public bodies because the matters being litigated concern legislation, policy and resource issues.

Furthermore, the policy of personalisation (see Chapter 9) will, in the government's view involve a careful weighing up by local authorities of the risks and benefits of giving a person more choice and control about how his or her needs should be met.[1] Local authorities will be more than mindful of the possible legal consequences of getting it wrong. They will be attempting, presumably, to steer a middle course between absurd and disproportionately restrictive approaches to risk at one extreme – and wildly hazardous risk taking at the other.

HEALTH AND SAFETY AT WORK LEGISLATION

Community care is affected by various health and safety at work duties. Breach of these duties can give rise to criminal offences prosecuted by, for example, the Health and Safety Executive; in addition, employees can sometimes bring civil law personal injury actions. There are duties towards non-employees as well as employees, on the basis of which health and safety prosecutions may be brought. It is beyond the scope of this book to enter into detail. However, there are one or two general points to be made.

DUTIES TO PROTECT EMPLOYEES AND NON-EMPLOYEES

A number of duties are held by employers towards employees. These include s.2 of the Health and Safety at Work Act 1974, the Management of Health and Safety at Work Regulations 1999, and the Manual Handling Regulations Operations 1992, etc. In addition, under s.3 of the 1974 Act, there is a duty on the employer to conduct its undertaking in such a way as to ensure, so far as is reasonably practicable, that non-employees who may be affected are not exposed to risks to their health and safety. For instance, when cardio-angiography treatment was not routinely checked before it was used, air got into the syringe and thence into the patient's bloodstream causing death. The Crown Court found an absence of a reasonably safe system of work under s.3.[2]

REASONABLE PRACTICABILITY IN HEALTH AND SAFETY: WEIGHING UP PEOPLE'S NEEDS AND STAFF SAFETY

The term 'reasonably practicable' recurs frequently in health and safety at work legislation, and is of pivotal importance. The traditional approach by the courts has been to weigh up the level of risk to employees against the cost of doing something about it in terms of resources, staffing, time

1   Department of Health (2007) *Independence, Choice and Risk*. London: DH.
2   *Health and Safety Executive v Norfolk and Norwich Healthcare NHS Trust* (1999) Crown Court.

and effort. If the cost involved would be clearly disproportionate to the risk, then it might not be reasonably practicable to eliminate or reduce the risk.[3]

However, when an employer is considering the reasonable practicability of reducing risk to its employees, it has to keep in mind the benefit or utility of the activity in question. For example, public bodies have both statutory duties to provide services and owe a common law duty of care to the public they serve. The courts have stated that, in some circumstances, the provision of certain services may entail a degree of risk to those delivering the service. This risk should not, however, be at an unacceptable level. This means a balance has sometimes to be struck between staff safety and the needs of service users. The service provider will have to make proportionate efforts to deliver the service without exposing its staff to unacceptable risk.

MANUAL HANDLING: PROPORTIONATE, BALANCED DECISION-MAKING

For instance, in the context of manually handling and physical transfers of people in health and social care, proportionality would suggest that the greater the needs of the service user, so the greater efforts have to made by the service provider to manage the risk at an acceptable level – before concluding that the service cannot be provided. This makes competent risk assessment of the individual situation essential, as pointed out both by the law courts[4] and the leading professional guidance on the subject.[5]

So, it was unlawful when a local authority failed to take into account a person's osteoporosis and the effect of hoisting on it, when applying an allegedly blanket policy about hoist use.[6] Equally, following such assessment, it would be unlawful and a criminal offence (under the health and safety at work legislation) to place staff at unacceptable risk, in order to meet needs in a hazardous manner – in one case, lifting a disabled boy at school manually in order to change incontinence pads.[7]

Thus, in a case about the manual handling of two women with learning disabilities the local authority had to weigh up such competing

3   *Edwards v National Coal Board* [1949] 1 All ER 743, Court of Appeal.

4   *R(A&B, X&Y) v East Sussex County Council (no.2)* [2003] EWHC Admin 167.

5   Smith, J. (ed.) (2005) *Guide to the Handling of People.* 5th edition. Teddington: Backcare.

6   *R(Clegg) v Salford City Council* [2007] EWHC 3276 Admin.

7   *K v X Grammar School Governors* [2007] EWCA Civ 165.

considerations. The court held that the rights of disabled people would not override those of paid carers and vice versa. Nevertheless, it might mean that in certain circumstances paid carers might have to work at higher, but not unacceptable, levels of risk – depending on the needs, and threat to the human rights, of a disabled person. The local authority would have to weigh up the women's wishes, feelings, reluctance, fear, refusal, dignity, integrity and quality of life, as well as the risk to staff.[8] Such balancing, and the taking of some, acceptable, risk by employees, has been referred to in other health and social care cases, including the making of beds in a disabled children's home,[9] bed transfers of a man with dementia in hospital,[10] and ambulance men answering an urgent call involving manual handling.[11]

These legal cases are consistent with Health and Safety Executive guidance. This has always pointed out that reasonable practicability does not entail that all risk be removed. Otherwise there would, for instance, be no adequate fire brigade.[12] Risk assessment must be performed in context. The Health and Safety Commission also has stated that, within the health service, some situations and activities will call for higher levels of risk taking. One such activity would be rehabilitation.[13]

CONTRACTING OUT SERVICES: RESPONSIBILITIES OF HEALTH OR SOCIAL CARE COMMISSIONER

A local authority or NHS body could be prosecuted for risks to the health and safety of an independent care provider's employees, as well as to that of service users, if those risks have arisen through failures in the contracting process.

For instance, in one case a local authority allocated inadequate funding to the contract. It also failed to check on the safety record of the contractor in question and to monitor the performance of the contract. Poor practice and unsafe working flourished, leading to two serious accidents to the care provider's staff. The Health and Safety Executive prosecuted, successfully, both the care provider and the local

---

8   R(A&B, X&Y) v East Sussex County Council (no.2) [2003] EWHC Admin 167.
9   Koonjul v Thameslink NHS Health Care Trust (2000) PIQR 123, Court of Appeal.
10   Urquhart v Fife Primary Care Trust [2007] CSOH 02, Court of Session, Scotland.
11   King v Sussex Ambulance Service [2002] EWCA Civ 953.
12   Health and Safety Executive (2004) Manual Handling: Manual Handling Operations Regulations 1992, Guidance on Regulations. 3rd edition. Sudbury: HSE, para 32.
13   Health Service Commission (1998) Manual Handling in the Health Services. London: HSC, p.43.

authority under, respectively, sections 2 and 3 of the Health and Safety at Work Act 1974.[14]

NEGLIGENCE

Negligence cases are brought in health and social care when people seek financial compensation for personal injury, usually physical, sometimes psychological. The legal test is whether there was a duty of care, whether it was breached and whether it caused the harm alleged. In many circumstances the duty of care owed by local authority and NHS staff will be straightforward – for instance, if there is a basic lapse in standards of care by medical doctors, or local authority care staff were to drop a person or supply defective equipment that caused an accident.[15]

However, the courts sometimes protect local services authorities and NHS bodies and say that, even if something has gone wrong, no duty of care is owed. They tend to provide such protection when they think there are complicated matters of policy, resources or sensitive decision-making involved – or if the alleged failure is entangled with statutory duties under legislation (such as assessment under the NHS and Community Care Act 1990).

For instance, when it was alleged that a social worker had failed to protect a couple with learning disabilities from being tortured by local youths, the courts said that even had she been at fault, no duty of care arose in any case.[16] Likewise the courts protected a local authority, when it was alleged that the late delivery of a piece of disability equipment (bed rails) by a local authority had been the cause of an accident (falling out of bed).[17] The NHS, too, will be protected, for instance, if it is a matter of lack of resources underpinning the failure of an ambulance service,[18] or an administrative and statutory framework underlying the failure in provision of mental health aftercare services.[19]

---

14 *Health and Safety Executive v London Borough of Barnet* (1997) unreported, Crown Court.

15 *Wyatt v Hillingdon London Borough Council* [1978] 76 LGR 727, Court of Appeal.

16 *X&Y v Hounslow London Borough Council* [2009] EWCA Civ 286.

17 *Sandford v Waltham Forest LBC* [2008] EWHC 1106 (QB).

18 *Kent v Griffiths* (2000) 3 CCLR 98, Court of Appeal.

19 *Clunis v Camden and Islington Health Authority* [1998] 3 All ER 180, Court of Appeal.

Index